Modernism, War, and Violence

NEW MODERNISMS SERIES

Bloomsbury's *New Modernisms* series introduces, explores, and extends the major topics and debates at the forefront of contemporary Modernist Studies.

Surveying new engagements with such topics as race, sexuality, technology, and material culture, and supported with authoritative further reading guides to the key works in contemporary scholarship, these books are essential guides for serious students and scholars of Modernism.

Published Titles

Modernism: Evolution of an Idea
Sean Latham and Gayle Rogers

Modernism in a Global Context
Peter J. Kalliney

Modernism, Science, and Technology
Mark S. Morrisson

Modernism's Print Cultures
Faye Hammill and Mark Hussey

Forthcoming Titles

Modernism and the Law
Robert Spoo

The Environments of Modernism
Alison Lacivita

Modernism, Sex, and Gender
Celia Marshik and Allison Pease

Modernism, War, and Violence

Marina MacKay

Bloomsbury Academic
An imprint of Bloomsbury Publishing Plc

B L O O M S B U R Y
LONDON • OXFORD • NEW YORK • NEW DELHI • SYDNEY

Bloomsbury Academic
An imprint of Bloomsbury Publishing Plc

50 Bedford Square
London
WC1B 3DP
UK

1385 Broadway
New York
NY 10018
USA

www.bloomsbury.com

BLOOMSBURY and the Diana logo are trademarks of Bloomsbury Publishing Plc

First published 2017

© Marina MacKay, 2017

Marina MacKay has asserted her right under the Copyright, Designs and Patents Act, 1988, to be identified as Author of this work.

All rights reserved. No part of this publication may be reproduced or transmitted in any form or by any means, electronic or mechanical, including photocopying, recording, or any information storage or retrieval system, without prior permission in writing from the publishers.

No responsibility for loss caused to any individual or organization acting on or refraining from action as a result of the material in this publication can be accepted by Bloomsbury or the author.

British Library Cataloguing-in-Publication Data
A catalogue record for this book is available from the British Library.

ISBN: HB: 978-1-4725-9006-0
PB: 978-1-4725-9007-7
ePDF: 978-1-4725-9009-1
ePub: 978-1-4725-9008-4

Library of Congress Cataloging-in-Publication Data
A catalog record for this book is available from the Library of Congress.

Series: New Modernisms

Cover design: Daniel Benneworth-Gray
Cover image © Getty Images/upsidedowndog

Typeset by Newgen Knowledge Works (P) Ltd., Chennai, India

To find out more about our authors and books visit www.bloomsbury.com. Here you will find extracts, author interviews, details of forthcoming events and the option to sign up for our newsletters.

CONTENTS

1 A terrible beauty is born 1
2 Modernism and the Great War 35
3 Modernism and political violence 61
4 Journeys to a war 85
5 Modernism and the Second World War 103

Epilogue: Cold War modernism? 131

Works cited 143
Bibliography 157
Index 163

1

A terrible beauty is born

> *More or less consciously Europe is preparing herself for a spectacle of much violence and perhaps of an inspiring nobility of greatness. And there will be nothing of what she expects.*
>
> JOSEPH CONRAD, "Autocracy and War" (83)

"You will be astonished to find how like art is to war, I mean 'modernist' art," announced the writer, artist, and master-publicist Wyndham Lewis early in *Blasting and Bombardiering*, his 1937 memoir of his time as a leading modernist agitator and a soldier and veteran of the First World War. "They talk a lot about how a war just-finished effects art," Lewis wrote, "[b]ut you will learn here how a war *about to start* can do the same thing. I have set out to show how war, art, civil war, strikes and coup d'états dovetail into each other" (4, emphasis in original).

The first purpose of this book, *Modernism, War, and Violence*, is similar to the one Lewis declares. It sets out to describe the connections between modernist literary culture and the virtually continuous public violence that shocked the age, although going beyond the period with which Lewis is concerned—he begins on the eve of the First World War and ends with Britain's General Strike in 1926—in order to consider anticipations and experiences of conflict in the late nineteenth century, and moving forward to the early Cold War, the famous age of anxiety in which modernism found itself institutionalized. But this book also outlines how critics in more recent decades have differently accounted for links between modernism and war, modernism and violence. Readers of modernism—and modernists themselves, as in the case of Lewis—have often sensed connections between the massive geopolitical shocks and the aesthetic upheavals of the first half of the twentieth century. From the coffin-shaking booms of Thomas Hardy's anticipatory "Channel Firing," a poem he wrote in April 1914 as the Great War approached, to the suspenseful dread of Samuel Beckett's Atomic-Age limbos, many modernist works have long since been understood by critics as, among many other things, responses to the world-shattering conditions of their times, and as works that enacted the trauma of those times through their signature transformations of established conventions of representation. Recounting the intertwined and competing stories that have been told about literary experiment and political upheaval across the early twentieth century, this book sets out to describe why so many critics have indeed found that, as Lewis suggested, modernism and war "dovetail into each other."

Modernism and war, modernism and violence

So why not just modernism and war? Why modernism, war, and *violence*? Violence is of course a precondition of war, and from any moral point of view, its most important aspect, given what war does to people (and to nonhuman animals and the environment). But there were forms of violence in this period that go far beyond traditional understandings of war, which is by convention and at least in theory, if only inconsistently in historical fact, bound by formalized rules. For example, war is meant not merely to happen but to be "declared" by one nation on another, wars are retrospectively corralled within dates such as 1914–18 or 1939–45, but modernists were also often deeply interested by forms of political violence that observe none of the formalities of war. The terror in terrorism, for example, is derived in substantial part from the fact that it appears to obey no obvious rules of engagement, and is liable to strike unpredictably: an arbitrariness that may help to explain its interest for modern writers on both sides of the Atlantic. On the eve of modernism, the late nineteenth century saw a wave of terrorist bombings and assassinations in the Britain Isles, the United States, and across the European continent. Invented in the 1860s (and patented by Alfred Nobel in 1867), dynamite was "a key development in the cultural and imaginative history of terror," particularly in view of the fact that it emerged alongside the burgeoning of a mass press that could disseminate far and wide its threat and its damage (Clymer 6–7). Dynamite quickly became associated with political revolutionaries, and especially with anarchists; a newspaper-fuelled moral panic ensued because, in the words of historian Antony Taylor, the figure of the *dynamitard* served as "a metaphor for the broader dissolution of European society" (46), a sense of dissolution that could be seen as the heart of literary modernism itself.

Emerging against the background of terroristic violence, modernism also took its course alongside other forms of violence. In the interwar years, and right across Europe, the whole idea of government was transformed by the rise of modern totalitarianism, beginning with the Russian Revolution in 1917, an event abetted by a utopian and visionary modernist intelligentsia that the political revolution then largely disavowed (Stites 6). With consequences that would shape the rest of the century, Mussolini took power in Italy in 1922, Stalin in Russia in 1924, and Hitler in Germany in 1933, but the triumph of authoritarian regimes can be seen almost everywhere in Europe between the wars, from General Pilsudski in Poland (in 1926) and General Franco in Spain (in 1939) to King Zog in Albania (in 1928) and King Carol in Romania (in 1938). In 1920, twenty-six of the twenty-eight European states were parliamentary democracies of some kind; by 1939, just twelve of them; by 1941, there were five (Lee, xi).

While this book is concerned primarily with violence between states or directed in some form against the state, particular regions such as the American South were also afflicted with other forms of violence, in many ways more repugnant and as lastingly damaging. Nancy Cunard's pioneering—and now much discussed—anthology *Negro* (1934) assembled an extraordinary mixture of writings by and about "the black race," and her foreword offered as the book's literal starting point the contemporary context of violence against black Americans:

> The reader finds first in this panorama the full violence of the oppression of the 14 million Negroes in *America* and the upsurge

of their demands for mere justice, that is to say their full and equal rights alongside of their white fellow-citizens. At no other time in the history of America have there been so many lynchings as in the past 2 years, so many "legal" murders, police killings and persecutions of coloured people. The Scottsboro frame-up [a miscarriage of justice after nine African American teenagers were falsely accused of raping two white women] is more than an attempt to electrocute 9 innocent black Alabamians—it is part of the effort to force into the dumbest and most terrorised form of subjection all Negro workers who dare to live otherwise than as virtual slaves. (iii)

Her foreword finishes with a denunciation of imperialism in Africa, "[a] continent in the iron grip of its several imperialist oppressors" (iv), and the final word in the anthology is given to a survey of the effects of colonization that is unambiguously titled "The White Man Is Killing Africa" (822–55) and that covers topics such as forced labor and police repression of Africans at the hands of white imperialists.

For many critics, it has become increasingly significant that modernism ran its course against the violence of empire and, finally, of decolonization. "Where are the boundaries, one might ask, between civil war, rebellion, revolution or insurgency?" asks Petra Rau, introducing a volume on modern war writing: "What is the difference between 'armed conflict,' 'hostilities' and 'war'?" (14). Her questions offer an important reminder of the definitional problems presented by violence that falls outside the conventionalized structures of war as such: "Indian Mutiny" versus "Sepoy Rebellion" versus "First Indian War of Independence," to give the famous Victorian example, and one that reminds us of modernism's own late imperial contexts. The implications of imperial decline have been addressed in a wide range of ways in modernist studies, from Jed Esty's influential argument that 1920s modernist pseudo-universality gives way to a new post-imperial concern with Englishness as merely one culture among others, to John Marx's suggestion that modernist narratives of imperial decline point toward a new cosmopolitanism producing more democratic conceptions of English as a resource available to the migrant and the marginal. But the late colonial context is especially relevant for thinking about modernism and violence, given the extent to which contested political sovereignty depends upon the threat or reality of force: "the fundamental point that terrorism as political violence is the ground upon which sovereignty is in many cases defined," as Elleke Boehmer and Stephen Morton put it (6).

To talk about modernism, war, and violence is to reflect the widening scope of how modernist studies has come to talk about cultural conflict, from the almost instantaneous identification of T. S. Eliot's *The Waste Land* (1922) as a response to the cataclysm of the Great War to, almost a hundred years on, our generally shared critical sense that the history of modernism as a whole intersects at many different points with world-scale transformations across half a century affecting many millions of people. This is why to think about modernism, war, and violence means registering many of the topics critics have brought to literary modernism as a whole in recent decades: questions about authorship and institutional status, for example, and about the relationship between formalism and historicism, and about class, gender, sexuality, race, empire, and region.

The year 1914 continues to be central to the story modernist studies tells about writers' interests in war and violence, but is no longer the whole of it. And so, to take a recent example, Sarah Cole's *At the Violet Hour* (2012) addresses modernism in relation to the two world wars but also alongside anarchist terror at the fin-de-siècle and the bloodshed associated with decolonization in Ireland in the following two decades. "It is astonishing," she writes, "how thoroughly the problematic of violence as an organizing cultural and aesthetic fact underwrote the literature of the years between 1890 and 1940" (4). Although perhaps Cole breaks off the story prematurely by ending in 1940, I obviously share her sense of the sheer pervasiveness of politically motivated violence in the period associated with modernism. Modernism records decades of bloodshed, carried out with deliberate intention, within nations and across continents, for ideological ends that cover what in retrospect looks like the full spectrum from the broadly defensible—in the sense that, as for the British in 1939, there are times when war becomes thinkable as the least worst option—to the kind of incomprehensibility of the Holocaust, an event that even a post-theological age could describe only in the language of evil.

If studies of modernism and twentieth-century war writing, once divided, have clearly come considerably to overlap, at the same time newer attention to modernism and the broader manifestations of state power encourage us to think about modernism's engagements with the threat and actuality of violence outside the rubrics of war writing. Mark Wollaeger's *Modernism, Media, and Propaganda* (2006), for example, reconstructs the state-led information culture that emerged around the Great War in order to argue that "modernism and propaganda are two sides of the same coin of modernity" (1). At the other end of the period, Thomas Davis's *The Extinct Scene: Late Modernism and Everyday Life* (2015) places the violence of the Second World War in the much wider context of the terminal destabilizing of Britain's superpower status. Furthermore, the emergence through the past decade of the interdisciplinary field of literature and human rights may prove to have particular importance for modernist studies given the significance of 1945, the year of the emergence of the United Nations, as a conventional endpoint in the periodizing of modernism; and the insights of human rights studies are already making themselves felt in work on modernism, violence, and the state by, for example, Janice Ho in *Nation and Citizenship in the Twentieth-Century British Novel* (2015). Considerations of modernism and violence now require us to go far beyond the canonical instance of the Great War, although *as* the canonical instance it serves as an essential place to start.

The Great War and the "origins" of modernism

One reason why I began with Wyndham Lewis's *Blasting and Bombardiering* is that, published in 1937, it shows how soon after the heyday of high modernism attempts were already being made to historicize literary experiment in relation to war. Writing as the prospect of another world war materialized, Lewis anchored modernism to the First World War, establishing a connection that continues to resonate in modernist studies. By the end of the twentieth century, the connection between the two "events" of modernism and the war had become a critical cliché of "nearly sacral character," as Vincent Sherry put it in *The Great War and the Language of Modernism* (2003) (6). Throughout the history of modernist studies, Sherry argues, critical assertions of the link between modernism and the First World War have operated as "a sort of ritual invocation, which serves to silence, not to stimulate and certainly not to organize, further inquiry" (7). The tenacity of this "ritual invocation" is one reason why we need to examine at the outset the range of assumptions upon which it rests, before turning (as the next chapter does) to how modernists actually wrote about the Great War. That the war had a powerful impact on modernist writers is virtually impossible to dispute; that the impact should be understood as directly causal, however, is a harder case to make.

To begin with Lewis, the means by which he links war and modernism follows the "great men" school of historiography, whereby historical outcomes are shaped by named individuals rather than impersonal political, social, or economic forces. According to the scenario Lewis outlines, a heroic band of avant-garde writers assembled by 1914 were ready to explode the fool's paradise of a complacent prewar English culture. Lewis influentially coined the term "Men of 1914" to refer to this group of modernists consisting of himself; T. S. Eliot; James Joyce; Ezra Pound; and the right-wing poet, translator, and essayist T. E. Hulme. (The least widely known name on Lewis's roster, Hulme had an important influence on a number of contemporaries although his death in action in 1917 brought his own career to an early end.) For Lewis in *Blasting and Bombardiering*, these 1914 modernists were "*the first men of a Future that has not materialized,*" and he characterizes the war's outbreak as the event that terminally foreclosed the modernist future that these writers' work had augured (256, emphasis in original). A "war about to start" had helped to create modernism, but the war that arrived had killed it.

This is modernism recast as a missed opportunity, and we might note at this point that Lewis is narrating modernist history in terms redolent of a familiar interwar motif: the fine flower of the nation cut off in its promising youth: "Strong eyes, fine limbs, haughty athletes," these men are, ironically, "[l]ess chanced ... for life" than the rat of Isaac Rosenberg's "Break of Day in the Trenches" (137). This is no unique instance of the leakage into modernist discourse of what had quickly become a mainstream cultural trope of doomed, beautiful young men. In the "Death by Water" section of *The Waste Land*, the reader is urged to recall the drowned Phlebas, "who was once handsome and tall as you" (65), while in Pound's *Hugh Selwyn Mauberley* (1920), the war has killed "a myriad, / And of the best, among them": this was "wastage as never before. / Young blood and high blood, / Fair cheeks, and fine bodies" (113).

Thanks to Gertrude Stein and Ernest Hemingway, a more distinctively American version of this motif survives in the cliché that casts the expatriate modernists in Paris as the "Lost Generation," reflecting, in Keith Gandal's words, "the disillusionment or the alienation from traditional values brought on by the crisis of the Great War or the failure of civilization it represented" (5). In fact, Gandal puts this particular cliché under serious pressure by proposing that it was not the war that actually scarred the canonical men of the American canon, Ernest Hemingway, F. Scott Fitzgerald, and William Faulkner, but their having missed out on it: "deemed unsuitable as candidates for full military service or command, and the result was that they felt themselves 'emasculated' ... not because of their encounters with trench warfare in a mechanized army or their consciousness of mass slaughter, but because either they got nowhere near the trenches or because they got to them in 'trivial,' noncombat roles" (5). Instead of a generation of modernists who had rejected normative prewar values, Gandal offers a group of men damaged by the fact that they had internalized the old values far too well.

Crucially, then, in telling the story of modernism and war as modernists themselves understood it, we might be mindful of the extent to which their self-understanding could not help but be informed by the culture from which it arose, even when its conscious orientation toward that culture was adversarial in many other ways. To observe that, for example, Lewis's lament for a modernism cut off in its prime reprises a mainstream trope of young men's promise cut tragically short is not to accuse Lewis of some sort of false consciousness or bad faith, but only to underscore that the historiography of modernism, as of any other cultural phenomenon, always speaks more or less audibly of the historical moments at which it emerged. War shaped modernism, but it also shaped ideas about modernism. We see this again in the way in which Lewis's historical vantage point leads him to find in the immediately prewar period a literary-historical version of the *belle époque* myth in which the postwar sense of depletion and disillusionment projects a nostalgic glow over the years before the catastrophe that gave them, by way of painful contrast, their seeming innocence and fecundity. Again, this is not simply a form of mystification, since, as some critics have shown, the postwar narrative of a modernism curtailed had some basis in historical actuality. In *London, Modernism, and*

1914 (2010), Michael Walsh reconstructs the extraordinary creative energy across literature and the visual arts during the months leading up to the war. He quotes Osbert Sitwell, a one-time Lewis ally and patron, as another witness to a prewar moment in which a "ferment such as I have never since felt in this country prevailed over the world of art. It seemed as if at last we were on the verge of a great movement" (4).

In response to Lewis's provocative claim about a modernism created and destroyed by war, we might point out that, with the necessary exception of the war casualty Hulme, the major works of Lewis's "Men of 1914" substantially postdated the war. Famously, it was 1922 that saw the publication of the most canonical of them all, *The Waste Land* and *Ulysses*, as well as Virginia Woolf's first experimental novel, *Jacob's Room*. From that point of view, the effect of the war on modernism appears more generative than destructive: modernism seems less a casualty of the war than one of the war's outcomes, and many critics have seen modernism not as a missed opportunity from the summer of 1914 but as among the cultural effects of an unprecedentedly traumatic war.

That said, the writers we associate most immediately with the First World War are not generally thought of as modernists. Literary experiment was no inevitable result of war experience—nor even an especially likely one, for that matter, given the poets who come to mind most immediately: Wilfred Owen, Ivor Gurney, and Siegfried Sassoon did not undertake wholesale renovations of the lyric and satirical forms they inherited from their precursors (although we might want to make an exception here for Rosenberg, some of whose war poems have a spare, laconic, imagistic quality that can feel very "modernist."). The longstanding distinction between writers who had experienced the war at first hand and those who had not is understandable given the insistence within the period's combatant writing on the incomprehensibility of combat experience to civilians. We see the most aggressive version of this phenomenon in Sassoon's poems, as when he fantasizes in "Blighters" about punishing the perceived jingo idiocies of civilians with mass slaughter in a music hall: "I'd like to see a Tank come down the stalls, / Lurching to rag-time tunes, or 'Home, sweet Home,' / And there'd be no more jokes in Music-halls / To mock the riddled corpses round Bapaume" (21). In a highly public attack on noncombatant ignorance in his "Soldier's Declaration," he denounced "the callous complacency with which the majority of those at home regard the continuance of the agonies which they do not share, and which they have not sufficient imagination to realise" (Egremont 144). This is why, Sassoon believed, civilians could condone the protraction of a profoundly costly war whose political objectives looked ever less clear as the war went on. A commitment to the uniqueness and non-transmissibility of the soldier's experience is what James Campbell has termed "combat gnosticism" in a trenchant essay of that title, where he describes how criticism on the literature of the Great War has unreflectively "formed itself around a certain set of aesthetic and ethical principles that it garners from its own subject" (203); and, as a result, tends uncritically to repeat the combatant writer's view that war experience "represents a qualitatively separate order of experience that is difficult if not impossible to communicate to any who have not undergone an identical experience" (204).

Borrowing from Campbell's insights, perhaps "combat gnosticism" explains why modernism and trench writing, notwithstanding their contemporaneous appearance, were historically treated as different traditions, requiring separate reading protocols. In *Writing War in the Twentieth Century* (2000), for example, Margot Norris sees the canons of modernism and war writing as distinct bodies of work, although she also offers the more pointed argument that modernism actively worked to supersede the writing of the trench poets. For Norris, the interwar period saw a contest between "conflicting aesthetics," and modernism declared its decisive victory over combatant writing with W. B. Yeats's notorious decision to exclude Owen from *The Oxford Book of Modern Verse* (1936) on the grounds that "passive suffering is not a theme for poetry" (Norris 37). While she goes on to describe a range of ways in which modern war and modern aesthetics overlapped as the century went on, Norris argues that modernism *as such* largely makes the dead of the First World War disappear. Thus, when modernist writers lament a brutal, wasteful war in poems like *Hugh Selwyn Mauberley*, what they are grieving is less the war than the lack of discrimination it showed in killing artists like Pound's sculptor friend Henri Gaudier-Brzeska (Norris 36).

The view that literary modernism and combatant writing are separate areas of study has a distinguished critical pedigree, and Campbell pays particular attention to Paul Fussell's classic *The*

Great War and Modern Memory (1975). An infantryman in the Second World War, Fussell dedicated the book to a dead comrade, as if to declare upfront his credentials for writing about war. Fussell used the trench writers to dismiss almost as a belated aside any connection between experimental aesthetics and war experience. The combatant writers with whom he was concerned were explicitly *not* modernists, but writers whose "stylistic traditionalism" (Fussell 313) rendered them "lesser talents" and "clearly writers of the second rank" (314); and of course it would be possible to take issue with this modernist-inflected use of formal experiment as the single measure of literary quality. Fussell writes that the "roster of major innovative talents who were not involved with the war is long and impressive. It includes Yeats, Woolf, Pound, Eliot, Lawrence, and Joyce—that is, the masters of the modern movement" (313–14). The assumption runs through *The Great War and Modern Memory* that First World War writing and modernist literary studies are really two different areas of inquiry, an assumption already in evidence as early as Bernard Bergonzi's *Heroes' Twilight*, first published ten years earlier.

It is "curiously difficult to consider war poetry and modernism in the same focus" writes Bergonzi in an appendix: "If *The Waste Land* is a great poem, then how valuable are Owen and Sassoon?" (227). Tellingly, this is a question that many people in modernist studies would no longer think to ask. That we experience no acute conflict between valuing Eliot and valuing Owen speaks to the dissolution of primarily formalist and evaluative readings of modernism and the acceptability, if not outright triumph, of historicist and nonevaluative modes for reading a period that, over a century after the Somme, feels historical in a way that could not have been the case for Bergonzi and Fussell's generation of critics.

This decisive historicist turn in modernist studies over the past twenty years has many important implications. For example, critical attention to publishing culture has revealed how modernism was understood in too isolated a way for much of its history ("the preservation of something called 'modernism' in intellectual amber" is how Michael North describes this phenomenon [1999: 11]), and so by reconstructing the literary environment of the 1910s and 1920s we come to see the different ways in which what became known as modernism cohabited at the time with other creative enterprises, including "war writing." For example, we would not necessarily expect to discover that it was the Woolfs' Hogarth Press that published war veteran Herbert Read's autobiographical *In Retreat* (1925), a story that, notwithstanding Read's links to forms of radicalism ranging from imagism to anarchism, is pure war reportage. And we would probably not expect to find this fragment of war documentary in the same series of Hogarth essays as Woolf's "Mr Bennett and Mrs Brown" and other works on modernist aesthetics such as Roger Fry's "The Artist and Psychoanalysis" and Robert Graves's "Contemporary Techniques of Poetry"—and Graves was, we recall, another war veteran, who would become known best to many readers from his Great War memoir, *Good-Bye to All That* (1929).

But a much further-reaching implication of the historicist emphasis in modernist studies is that we tend to have no difficulty in accepting that the effects of the First World War were felt among a much larger population of writers than those who had experienced the war in uniform, and that even the most civilian of modernists were working in a social and cultural environment saturated and transformed by total war. Over the past twenty years, a significant body of scholarship has emerged with the aim of "negotiating the space between modernism and the First World War," as Allyson Booth puts it in the subtitle to her influential *Postcards from the Trenches* (1996). Focusing in particular on how modernist writing in the 1910s and 1920s complicates ideas of place, perception, and embodiment, Booth finds that these ideas were being transformed at the very same time on the Front:

> [E]ven at moments when the spaces of war seem most remote, the perceptual habits appropriate to war emerge plainly; that the buildings of modernism may delineate spaces within which one is forced to confront both war's casualties and one's distance from those casualties; that the dislocations of war often figure centrally in modernist form, even when war itself seems peripheral to modernist content. (4)

A representative instance of how this kind of argument works is Booth's dazzling chapter on "corpselessness" in which she reads Woolf's *Jacob's Room*—the peculiarly absent protagonist Jacob Flanders is named as such because he is marked out as one of the war's as-if-predestined victims—in relation to the absent bodies of wartime Britain. These bodies are absent in the sense that soldiers' remains were not brought home from the continent; they are visually absent owing to the prohibition on the dissemination of images of the British dead; most horrifyingly of all, they are absent in consequence of new military technologies that could effect the body's comprehensive and instantaneous dissolution, with the result that "huge numbers of soldiers simply disappeared" (Booth 29). More recently, Pearl James has offered similar insights into the canonical modernism of the United States, describing how works by writers such as Fitzgerald and Faulkner "reveal, refigure, omit, and aestheticize the violent death of young men" (9): on her reading, Fitzgerald's *The Great Gatsby* (1925) is a novel that "repeats one of the central experiences of war—losing a comrade" (26), as Nick Carraway makes the "attempt to assimilate the death of a fellow veteran, Jay Gatsby" (27), while "the central issue" of Faulkner's *Sartoris* (1929), in which a man returns from the war without his fighter pilot twin, is "the problem of mourning without a body" (18).

This sense that the literary impact of the war extends far beyond the work of soldier poets is surely what Trudi Tate has in mind when she characterizes modernism as "a peculiar but significant form of war writing" in a book that reads modernist fiction alongside the work of the trench writers (3). This is an important insight because even if we hesitate to identify modernism with any single historical provocation in a period of upheaval across so many areas of public and private life—modernism is also "a peculiar but significant" way of writing about empire, gender, environment, and many other topics—what Tate captures here is the extent to which modernist writing both changes and expands what we think it means for a literary work to be "about" something. And so, for example, with its elegiac meditations on grief and transience, on generational rupture, and the irretrievability of the early-twentieth-century past, as we read Woolf's *To the Lighthouse* (1927) we are already encouraged to apprehend the novel as a work "about" the First World War long before we learn that among the sudden and brutal losses the novel recounts in its lacerating middle section is that of the Ramsays' gifted son Andrew, one of "[t]wenty or thirty young men ... blown up in France" (181).

War as watershed

Woolf's treatment of the war in *To the Lighthouse* as a narrow "corridor" joining the irrecoverable past of the novel's first half to the altered postwar present of the novel's ending—the tripartite structure of the book was to be "Two blocks joined by a corridor," Woolf wrote in a note to herself—anticipates the most common way in which critics have characterized the relationship between war and modernism, as one of transformation (*Holograph* 48). On this model, national cultures entered the "corridor" of the war and came out as something quite different from their older selves; this major cultural crisis the war precipitated in European life led to the overhaul of established forms in literature and the other arts. This view of modernism in history accords with that of Lewis, who had expressed in a characteristically memorable way his belief that the Great War had been a watershed event for everyone who lived through it: "The War is such a tremendous landmark that locally it imposes itself upon our computations of time like the birth of Christ." Lewis writes: "We say 'pre-war' and 'post-war,' rather as we say B.C. or A.D." (*Blasting* 1). (Perhaps significantly, his universalizing first-person plural makes no distinction between former servicemen like himself and the civilians among his readership.)

Among all the readers who have anchored modernism as a change of sensibility to the First World War, Modris Eksteins has probably gone furthest. In his pan-European cultural history *Rites of Spring: The Great War and the Birth of the Modern Age* (1989), Eksteins narrates the events surrounding the sensational opening night in Paris on May 29, 1913 of Igor Stravinsky's experimental *The Rite of Spring*, the starting point for his striking claim that any causal relationship between modernism and the Great War needs to be understood as reciprocal. That is: even if the war helped to create modernism, modernists also helped to create the war, and they did so with an art that cast their complacent culture as fit for wholesale obliteration (this was to be "a war of liberation ... from the hypocrisy of bourgeois form and convenience" [Eksteins xv]) at the same time as they fetishized the regenerative power of killing—an important motif in James Frazer's influential *The Golden Bough* (1890) and Jessie Weston's *From Ritual to Romance* (1920) where rites of spring are regenerative stories of stylized killing and resurrection. "Horror was turned into spiritual fulfillment," Eksteins elaborates, "War became peace. Death, life. Annihilation, freedom. Machine, poetry. Amorality, truth" (202). In short, war becomes emancipation, and a radical purgative for the sickness modernism identified: the sickness of, in Pound's famous complaint, "an old bitch gone in the teeth, a botched civilisation" (*Mauberley* 113). George Bernard Shaw also took this line just after the war in his play *Heartbreak House* (1919), where the heartbreak house of the title stands for the whole of leisured prewar Europe: "an economic, political, and ... moral vacuum" (Shaw 2).

It is tempting to see such denunciations of prewar culture as the axiomatically questionable historiography of wisdom after the event, where the fact of its ending in catastrophe implies a necessarily harsh judgment on what that culture had inherently been. Nonetheless, it is easy to find evidence of contemporary feelings of decadence prior to the postwar judgment—this recurring sense that violence might be the answer to Europe's perceived predicament. We find it in, for example, the memorable "blasting" and "blessing" of Lewis's short-lived *BLAST* (1914–15): "an avenue for all those vivid and violent ideas that could reach the Public in no other way" Lewis wrote in the first of the magazine's two issues (n.p.); in the curses of the Italian Futurists on a European continent turned into a decayed museum ("We will glorify war—the world's only hygiene—militarism, patriotism, the destructive gesture of freedombringers, beautiful ideas worth dying for" [Marinetti 42]); and in Yeats's sense of the creative effects of conflict: "I think that all noble things are the result of warfare; great nations and classes, of warfare in the visible world, great poetry and philosophy, of invisible warfare, the division of a mind within itself, a victory, the sacrifice of a man to himself" ("Synge" 233). Or, for that matter, we can find it in the notorious 1914 lines from Rupert Brooke—not exactly a name to conjure with from the point of view of modernism—in which he contemplated his generation turning to war "as swimmers into cleanness leaping, / Glad from a world grown old and cold and weary" (19). There is clearly much to be said in favor of Eksteins's argument that the war had been imaginatively prepared for by prewar denunciations of a perceived cultural decadence, and with war as some sort of kill-or-cure remedy. Or war *and* modernism as remedy, rather, recalling the Futurists again: "Except in struggle, there is no more beauty. No work without an aggressive character can be a masterpiece. Poetry must be conceived as a violent attack on unknown forces, to reduce and prostrate them before man" (Marinetti 41). This is modernism as what in military terms would be the desperate policy of scorched earth, and it obviously supports Eksteins's sense of an artistic militarization of prewar high culture.

However, other critics have either linked modernism and the Great War in ways that are more geographically particular than Eksteins's presentation of violent pan-continental ferment; or, as Booth explicitly does, they have refused altogether to propose "specific cause-and-effect relationships," preferring instead to focus on the contemporary "perceptual equipment" that modernists and war writers shared (Booth 5). Undoing the old divisions between the concerns of First World War studies and modernist studies has been a major feature of critical work in the twenty-first century. One example would be the way in which Santanu Das's focus on "touch and intimacy in First World War literature" in his superb book of that title—which focuses on the experience of soldiers and war nurses—resonates in Cole's attention to the haptic in *At the Violet Hour*, a study of civilian modernism, with its early discussion of the pandying scene in Joyce's 1916 novel *A Portrait of the Artist as a Young Man* (Cole 8–12). In her earlier *Modernism, Male Friendship, and the First World War* (2003), Cole traces through the fiction of noncombatants such as Joseph Conrad, D. H. Lawrence, and E. M. Forster thematic concerns with male intimacy that recall the comradeship that so famously serves in war writing as the only redemptive aspect of life in the trenches: "a kind of standard, as well as a metaphor, for the most resilient, cherished, and vulnerable of bonds" (6). The historicist turn in modernist studies has brought First World War writing and modernism ever closer.

This is also true of studies of the origins of modernism in relation to the war. In contrast to Eksteins's dramatic continental transformation, Sherry's study of English public culture presents a much more localized and archival argument in support of the idea that the war helped to bring literary modernism into being. In *The Great War and the Language of Modernism*, the London-based modernists (Sherry's main case studies are the American-born Eliot and Pound and the English-born feminist dissident Woolf) were responding in what almost amounts to a satirical way to a language placed under virtually terminal strain by parliamentary and journalistic discourses contorting to defend a continental civil war—the national cost of which had quickly become apparent—that Britain should never have entered. On Sherry's reading, modernism's signature linguistic difficulty both mimics and mocks the false logic, the pseudo-rationality, of the period's outpouring of journalistic prose, a whole body of public argument attempting to legitimize a war marked by incoherent political causes and harrowing human effects.

But there is no straightforward critical consensus on claims about the First World War as the singularly modernist war, whether by that we mean a war that was broadly modernizing in its impact on the cultures that fought it, or a war in which we might find the origins of the specific artistic transformations of the 1920s. For Jay Winter, focusing on the social and imaginative structures through which Europeans reckoned with their losses, the cultural repercussions of the First World War were anything but "modernist." As he shows in his moving cultural history *Sites of Memory, Sites of Mourning* (1995), the war's traumatic progress appears not, as received wisdom has it, to have led to a wholesale rejection of prewar conventions but to a widespread revival of traditional and sacralizing forms, from spiritualism and other forms of superstitious or anti-positivistic thinking to the ancient practice of building monuments and memorials to the dead. Taking particular issue with Fussell's canonical identification of post-1918 modernity with the seemingly endless ironies thrown up by the war, Winter argues that this "cutting edge of 'modern memory', its multi-faceted sense of dislocation, paradox, and the ironic, could express anger and despair, and did so in enduring ways; it was melancholic, but it could not heal" (5). For Winter, consequently, there is something "misleading" and "tendentious" (5) about literary critics' emphasis on the war as a modernizing force when traditional artistic and social forms of mourning did not simply persist but demonstrably accrued new power in a culture devastated by mass death: "[t]he Great War, the most 'modern' of wars, triggered an avalanche of the 'unmodern' " (54).

However, we need not think in terms of either/or, for this critical divergence on the relative significance of the Great War for thinking about the emergence of modernism—and the competing claims are underpinned by a compelling wealth of critical insight and archival evidence on both sides—is not what it seems. The sticking point is not a disagreement about how people actually responded to the war but, rather, an underlying lack of consensus about definitions of modernism. For Sherry, modernism was always an elite form, a movement and a sensibility that achieved "equivalent privilege," as he puts it, to that of the political sphere whose verbal contortions it derided through mock-logical languages of its own; by this move, Sherry rejects Winter's attribution to modernist critics the view that modernism was a culturally representative force, enjoying "majority status" and "populist provenance" and thus altogether in tune with the popular life of its time rather than operating in its own autonomous or even oppositional sphere (*Language of Modernism* 19). There is no obvious way to cut through this impasse precisely because the question of how far modernism should be understood in relation to the mass or mainstream culture of its time has been fundamental to many of the central debates in modernist studies for at least the past twenty years.

But regardless of whether we understand modernism as altogether representative or downright unrepresentative of its culture at large—or somewhere between those distant extremes—most would agree that a number of the artistic strategies and psychosocial orientations we associate with literary modernism were more than merely incipient in the period leading up to 1914, and can be found in the work of writers considerably older than the major modernists whose work we associate with the 1920s. Conrad, to take perhaps the most straightforwardly canonical example, was approaching the end of his career by the time the war was over; he turned sixty-five in that modernist *annus mirabilis* of 1922, and died two years later. Yet throughout his major turn-of-the-century work we see a markedly modernistic handling of narrative form accompanied by confrontations with violence that elicit a powerful questioning of the social, psychological, and epistemological givens of his time, a kind of questioning that we typically associate with the post-1918 modernist icons. Registering the rich, problematic modernity of substantially prewar writers like Conrad (or Henry James or Ford Madox Ford) suggests that there are limits to any strictly causal account of modernism's relationship to the First World War, and that the emergence of modernism is obviously nowhere near as datable as its long-standing identification with the Great War implies. Although I shall return in the next chapter to the ways in which modernists responded to the war with what proved to be among the most enduring landmarks of twentieth-century literature, it is worth turning briefly beforehand to the relationships among modernism, war, and violence that emerged prior to 1914.

Before the Great War

One reason to consider the years before 1914 is to remind ourselves that even if we were considering British circumstances alone, the Great War was neither the first nor the only culturally traumatic war of the early twentieth century. Even as the nineteenth century turned into the twentieth, Britain was at war—and a war that it stood a worrying chance of losing at that—against the Boers in South Africa (1899–1902). In looking even briefly at literature around the turn of the century, we are compelled to notice, too, that the Great War was not even the first war in which can be heard the characteristically "modern" note of disillusioned antiwar feeling traditionally associated with writing after 1914.

For example, we already find that distinctively ironic feeling for the futilities of war in Hardy's 1902 poem "The Man He Killed." A West Country soldier in the Boer War reflects on the absurdity of his deathly combat with a working-class man from whom only nationality divides him, someone he considers much more likely to have been a drinking companion than a mortal enemy had they met in any other circumstances:

> "I shot him dead because—
> Because he was my foe,
> Just so: my foe of course he was;
> That's clear enough; although
>
> "He thought he'd 'list, perhaps,
> Off-hand like—just as I –
> Was out of work—had sold his traps—
> No other reason why.
>
> "Yes; quaint and curious war is!
> You shoot a fellow down
> You'd treat if met where any bar is,
> Or help to half-a-crown." (258–9)

In the first of these stanzas, the rhyme underscores the arbitrariness of the other soldier's death: following "foe" with "so" implies necessity, dictating in an almost meretriciously slick way that by virtue of being a "foe," he must be killed ("so"), but the more hesitant rhyme of "so" and "although" reveals the falsity of this pretended inevitability. This "although" introduces an equivalence vastly more profound than the fake equivalence of "he was my foe" and "so [I had to kill him]," for Hardy is emphasizing the more substantial likeness of two ordinary working men who have enlisted in the army in hard economic times without any political stake in the causes for which they fight ("no other reason why"). Or, in another contemporary piece of ventriloquism, Rudyard Kipling had a Boer War soldier wonder "What *is* the sense of 'ating those / 'Oom you are paid to kill?" (Kendall 35).

Hardy and Kipling were writing about professional soldiers, which explains the recurrence of monetary concerns in these poems—"out of work," "half a crown," "paid to kill"—and if writers who came later in the century found war so compellingly terrible a topic, it might well have been because the First World War was the first in which, from the British author's point of view, the nation's wars were no longer to be fought and endured at a considerable distance and by someone else—or, more bluntly, by people of lower social class and cultural attainment. Still, the sense these Boer War poems convey of the interchangeable status of killer and killed, of ally and enemy, becomes a central trope of the poetry of the world wars and of the work of civilian modernists (although "civilian modernists" is an awkward formulation when most of the canonical combatant writers of the two world wars were only ever temporary servicemen, civilians in uniform). Its most famous iteration is the hallucinatory postmortem encounter of Owen's "Strange Meeting": "I am the enemy you killed, my friend" (36). And it has been suggested that Eliot is rehearsing this trope in *The Waste Land* when the speaker hails his old comrade Stetson ("You who were with me in the ships at Mylae" [55]); and twenty years later in his Blitz poem "Little Gidding" (1942), when, in the aftermath of an air raid, the speaker encounters "a familiar compound ghost / Both intimate and unidentifiable" (203). So much for "unidentifiable," most critics note his resemblance to figures such as Yeats and Mallarmé, but, as Peter Middleton describes in an essay on "the ghosts of modernism," Eliot's air-raid specter also evokes a whole range of Great War apparitions from Owen's "enemy" to the dead officer Evans in Woolf's *Mrs Dalloway* (1925).

This encounter between the living man and his war-dead double becomes commonplace in Second World War poetry. The British speaker of Keith Douglas's "*Vergissmeinnicht*" stands over the putrefying corpse of a German soldier who nearly killed him in a battle on the same stretch of Tunisian desert a few weeks earlier, in a poem in which the links between the dead soldier and the living witness—who may also have been his killer, although the speaker is unsurprisingly vague on this point—prove incalculably stronger than anything tying either man to the nation or cause for which he fights. Also writing from the North African theater, the Scottish Gaelic modernist Sorley MacLean contemplates in "Death Valley" the body of the enemy. As in "*Vergissmeinnicht*," the materiality of death neutralizes the political cause behind that death when a pathetic young corpse lying among the rubbish of war on the dirty sand gives the lie to the bellicose propaganda alluded to in MacLean's epigraph, which tells us that "Some Nazi or other has said that the Fuehrer had restored to German manhood the 'right and joy of dying in battle'" (211). Obviously, much of what we think of as characteristic of Great War thinking resonates deep into the century. More importantly, though, it has a history going back to the late Victorian period.

That is to say, if MacLean's casual dismissal of the Nazi rhetoric recalls Owen's iconic demolition of the Latin dictum about the propriety of dying for one's country, the point Owen himself was making about the irrelevance of political causes in the degrading face of death can already be seen in, once again, Hardy's poetry of the Boer War. Written in 1902, Hardy's "Drummer Hodge" tells of the unceremonious interment—"Uncoffined – just as found"—in the dry South African soil of a young West Country soldier who has died in a country he does not know and, by implication, for a cause he cannot understand well enough to share:

> Young Hodge the Drummer never knew—
>   Fresh from his Wessex home—
> The meaning of the broad Karoo,
>   The Bush, the dusty loam,
> And why uprose to nightly view
>   Strange stars amid the gloam. (257)

Given how insistent commentators on modern war writing have been about the uniquely disenchanting effects of the First World

War, it is salutary to find as early as the turn of the century, in the literature of colonial wars, so many of the attitudinal habits we associate with the ostensible awakening of 1914.

Come the First World War, Kipling's son John ("Jack"), lost at Loos in 1915, would be among the half-million or so British war dead whose remains either disappeared or were never identified. Among Kipling's short stories about this war, the most canonical, "Mary Postgate"(1915) and "The Gardener" (1925), undertake a deeply ambiguous interrogation—indeed, perhaps more ambiguous than Kipling intended—of the psychopathologies of civilian grief that could easily have come from a modernist writer. English civilian Mary Postgate finds herself in a position where she can kill a German fighter pilot to avenge a bomb he may or may not have dropped on her village; the protagonist of "The Gardener" mourns a young man who may or may not be her illegitimate son. In both stories, Kipling captures states of half-volition and self-unknowing in relation to mourning similar to those described in stories by war-bereaved modernists like Katherine Mansfield. His poetry of the war's end, too, offers a self-lacerating version of what would become a virtually canonical critique of the war in the 1920s: "If any question why we died, / Tell them, because our fathers lied," Kipling wrote in one of his "Epitaphs of the War" (324); in another, a jingo politician reflects at the moment of his death on how he "lied to please the mob" in wartime:

> Now all my lies are proved untrue
> And I must face the men I slew.
> What tale shall serve me here among
> Mine angry and defrauded young? (324)

The language of fraud reappears among writers associated with modernism: "Then close your ears with dust and lie / Among the other cheated dead," Yeats wrote in his bitter "Reprisals," written in 1920 and withheld from publication in his lifetime, and addressed to the dead son of his patroness Lady Gregory (Foster 183). "Reprisals" is a far cry from the others he wrote about the late Major Robert Gregory, and also from his stubborn 1915 effort "A Reason for Keeping Silent" or "On Being Asked for a War Poem": "I think it better that in times like these /A poet's mouth be silent, for in truth / We have no gift to set a statesman right" (175).

This enraged pity for the "angry and defrauded young," "the ... cheated dead," has far-reaching significance for thinking about the cultural meanings of the war in relation to modernism. Samuel Hynes describes this significance in *A War Imagined: The First World War and English Culture* (1990), where he identifies a recurrent motif that he sums up as "the theme of the Old Men—the conviction that the war had empowered the elderly to send the young to their deaths" (246). Sassoon's poem "The Fathers" is characteristically explicit:

> Snug at the club two fathers sat,
> Gross, goggled-eyed, and full of chat.
> One of them said: "My eldest lad
> Writes cheery letters from Bagdad.
> But Arthur's getting all the fun
> At Arras with his nine-inch gun." (74)

One of these "impotent old friends" laments with wholly sincere stupidity that a third son hasn't seen action yet (75). Hynes saw in this narrative of young men slaughtered by their deluded elders a license for modernists to reject the past, and we see its impact in the insistent generation-consciousness that the modernists introduced into twentieth-century literary culture. The only unusual aspect of Kipling's use of the trope of the old men is that he is turning it against himself as a former propagandist, too old to fight but too ready to use his cultural authority to encourage others to enlist.

But—and here we need to look back to the start of the century again—if Kipling's sardonic denunciation of the causes of the war ("because our fathers lied") is most pronounced in the work he produced after the death of his youngest child, it is nonetheless hard to ignore the biting humor of some of his much earlier writings about the colonial wars he had presumably also supported at the time. These wars are, in the title of a poem from 1892, "The Widow's Party"—the "widow" is Queen Victoria, the so-called Widow at Windsor, and the "party" is not only the Company that is sent into battle, but also the murderous carnival of a battle that slaughters half of that Company by the end of the poem. There is good reason why Kipling should have returned to sight in recent decades as a complex and humane writer, and no longer the embodiment of a jingoism for which his name was once a byword. (Famously, he was among those of odious politics whom time has "[p]ardoned ... for writing well," in the patronizing verdict of W. H. Auden in 1939's "In Memory of W. B. Yeats" [82]) On the contrary, as Tim Kendall writes in his stylish survey of modern English war poetry, Kipling's poetry "can be tentative, self-doubting, and compassionate" (30).

Among the most enduring literary legacies of the First World War is the association of war poetry with antiwar feeling, but there are compelling critiques of militarism in other literary forms, and, again, from well before the war. In drama, for example, the Anglo-Irish George Bernard Shaw eschewed British imperial contexts and turned instead to the Serbo-Bulgarian war of 1885 (quite recent, but to a London audience probably a somewhat Ruritanian affair in the figurative as well as geographical sense). Critically and commercially successful, *Arms and the Man* (1894) is primarily a witty demolition of traditional notions of military glory, and the play hints at the moral direction war writing would take in the coming decades when it dramatizes the impassable gap between the heroic romance and the bloody actuality of soldiering. "How horrible!" gasps heroine Raina, fiancée of a dense Bulgarian war hero who is quixotically in thrall to the military myth; to which her soldier interlocutor responds, "And how ridiculous! Oh war! war! the dream of patriots and heroes! A fraud ... A hollow sham" (87). Formally, *Arms and the Man* is a relatively conventional satirical comedy, but it is significant nonetheless because of how explicitly it debunks at this early date the martial fantasies against which we are usually tempted to define the undeluded, disenchanted, and knowing modern attitude to war.

There are certainly more obviously modernist, and perhaps more searching, instances of turn-of-the-century writing that dismantle the quasi-heroic view of war that too easily gets associated with the period prior to 1914 to convey the unprecedented disempowerments of the trenches. And so, to turn from poetry and drama to prose fiction, the First World War is typically thought of as eliciting a body of writing exploring, in the years accompanying the transformative emergence of psychoanalysis, the mind-shattering effects of war on the men who fight, but we can find similar concerns in prewar literature. Following the experiences of a young Union private in the American Civil War, Stephen Crane's *The Red Badge of Courage* (1895) is among the most canonical treatments in the pre-1914 period of the psychic conflict between the exigencies of visceral fear and the forms of socialization that teach men to see military courage as an unqualified virtue, but more representative, in an anticipatory way, of the kind of shell-shock narrative associated with the 1920s is the representation of war damage in Lawrence's "The Shadow in the Rose Garden." First published in March 1914, when war with Germany was expected but not inevitable, the story opens with the thoroughly unwarlike scenario of a couple on their honeymoon. The husband, an electrician in the coalmines, and his socially aspirational wife find themselves at a Yorkshire seaside village where the bride once had a sexual relationship with a man of higher social standing. Her secretly sentimental journey results in psychological and ultimately marital breakdown after she meets her former lover again, as she had hoped. Now an invalided army officer, he does not recognize her because his mind is blasted by what would later be termed shellshock, sustained when he "went out to fight in Africa" (137). This long-standing object of social and erotic nostalgia is now "a handsome, soldierly fellow, and a lunatic" (133). The bride looks into his unseeing eyes and feels that he is barely a human being anymore, in an uncanny image of body without mind that prefigures the literary veterans of the First World War. Or, at least, it anticipates the veterans who populate modernist literature, for their attention to the complexities of consciousness tends to lead modernist writers to substitute psychiatric damage for the differently distressing visual evidence of combat. As historian Joanna Bourke forcefully demonstrates, physical disfigurement was a highly public feature of life after a war in which "the dismembered man became Everyman" (16), and when "[m]ass-mutilation was there for all to see" (35). Where specifically physical rather than solely psychological war injury has been inflicted upon modernism's war veterans, it tends to be overtly symbolic but not visually unsettling: Great War veterans like the impotent Jake Barnes in Ernest Hemingway's *The Sun Also Rises* (1926) and the wheelchair-using Harry Heegan in Sean O'Casey's play *The Silver Tassie* (1928) suffer from injuries that matter mainly because they entail supposedly emasculating sexual impairment, such as that of the disabled veteran Sir Clifford Chatterley in Lawrence's final novel.

Other stories published in *The Prussian Officer* (1914), the prewar collection in which "The Shadow in the Rose Garden" appeared, reveal Lawrence's attention to the debilitating effects of militarism. Along with his ominously titled series of prewar articles,

"In Fortified Germany," the stories "The Prussian Officer" and "The Thorn in the Flesh" are set during the Prussian military maneuvers Lawrence had seen when visiting the garrison town of Metz with his future wife Frieda Weekley (Frieda, née von Richthofen, was the daughter of a German career officer). The main character in each story is a young soldier at the mercy of the army's institutionalized bullying. In "The Thorn in the Flesh," an inexperienced soldier is taunted when his nerve breaks on a high rampart and he lashes out at his officer in visceral panic. In the extraordinary work of psychosexual symbolism "The Prussian Officer," a young orderly is persecuted by an infatuated superior whom he finally murders, effectively putting an end to his own life in doing so. Conventional ideals of manliness that get tested to destruction will become a familiar theme in the writing of the First World War—here, we might think of Woolf's traumatized Septimus Warren Smith, cautioned by the doctors in *Mrs Dalloway* that he is giving his Italian wife "a very odd idea of English husbands" (120), or of the shell-shocked Chris Baldry in Rebecca West's *The Return of the Soldier* (1918), whose masculine role requires that he be restored to sanity and dispatched to his likely death in France. But it is instructive to note the prevalence of this theme of beleaguered manliness in the prewar literature of colonial crisis. In Conrad's *Lord Jim* (1902), most famously, the virtuous title character makes what prove to be suicidally brave efforts at redemption through combat for a single catastrophic moment of cowardice.

Late imperial apocalypse

Violence is a recurrent theme of Conrad's fiction, and many critics have pointed out the common ground he shares with late Victorian adventure fiction. What is particularly interesting about this overlap between Conrad and imperial romance in the light of Nicholas Daly's account of how "the romance was presented as restoring the manhood of British fiction" (19), and Cole's summary of late-Victorian adventure as "a tradition of writing by, for, and about men and boys" (*Male Friendship* 96), is the insistent way in which Conrad uses violent colonial situations as an opportunity to question a range of masculine ideals connected to courage and stoicism, rather than (as in the adventure stories to which he is indebted) plot pretexts for his characters to display these values. And these colonial settings are inevitably violent, for as John McClure points out in his *Late Imperial Romance* (1994) violence is in fact a structural necessity of imperial romance: "For romance, as a moment's reflection suggests, *requires* ... a world at war—starkly divided, partially wild and mysterious, dramatically dangerous" (2–3). Following prior romancers, Conrad's questioning of masculine standards in imperial contexts exploits the frisson attendant on the unique vulnerability of selfhood when extracted from the social background that shores it up through elaborate systems of validation and punishment, or "the holy terror of scandal and gallows and lunatic asylums" (*Heart of Darkness* 60).

At the same time as Conrad was depicting violent crisis abroad, a more popular writer whom he admired was targeting colonial complacencies about the solidity of the ground beneath English feet. In H. G. Wells's *The War of the Worlds* (1897) a Martian invasion almost results in the destruction of humanity, which is to be enslaved as a source of food. This invasion, the narrator explains, "has robbed us of that serene confidence in the future which is the most fruitful source of decadence" and "left an abiding sense of doubt and insecurity in my mind" (185). *The War of the Worlds* is a violent colonial novel in reverse, with the complacent British now to be subjected to the dehumanizing treatment they have meted out to others:

> And before we judge of [the Martians] too harshly we must remember what ruthless and utter destruction our own species has wrought, not only upon animals, such as the vanished bison and the dodo, but upon its own inferior races. The Tasmanians, in spite of their human likeness, were entirely swept out of existence in a war of extermination waged by European immigrants, in the space of fifty years. (5)

The language of "inferior races" and "human likeness" reminds us that, as in the almost contemporary *Heart of Darkness* (1899), an anticolonial statement is not necessarily the same thing as an antiracist one. Still, it is certainly the case that Wells's dramatization of the colonial structure in *The War of the Worlds* must have been chillingly recognizable to its first readers, from the first exploratory invasion to the preliminary work of what in the era of imperial policing was euphemized as "pacification" ("They do not seem to have aimed at extermination so much as at complete demoralization and the destruction of any opposition" [105]) to the routing of the Martians at the hands of a hostile environment where they discover only belatedly that they have no immunity to local conditions, a phenomenon familiar from the history of failed colonial ventures. Writing of the prevalence of the invasion narrative in the twenty years leading up to the First World War, Bergonzi intriguingly speculates that "a subconscious fear of invasion and occupation," which these texts must have fuelled as well as reflected, "is perhaps why so many Englishmen reacted as if it were England herself that was being invaded, rather than Belgium" when the First World War finally materialized (*Heroes' Twilight* 23).

Although it is impossible to deny Wells's turn-of-the-century novels their status as significant precursors for thinking about the coming century's world wars—his 1908 *The War in the Air* anticipates a German effort at global domination, as well as apprehending with Wells's celebrated technological prescience that the wars of the near future will bring violence raining down from the skies—it may seem counterintuitive to invoke Wells in any discussion of modernism. It is still the case that many students of modernism will encounter his name (but seldom his actual fiction) only as a figurehead for the Edwardian generation whose work the modernists were reacting against—or perhaps not so much a figurehead, to change metaphors, as a straw man. Famously, he was among the "materialists" of Woolf's essay "Modern Fiction," responsible for the dominance of what she considered well-constructed but lifeless traditional novels (286). Woolf would have been thinking of his big realist novels of the Edwardian period rather than his science fiction, but what Wells's more seemingly fantastical fiction shows is the emergence of a new reportage style for addressing violence. Notwithstanding the conventional, Woolf-inspired exclusion of his work from considerations of modernism, it is here, in relation to the writing of late-imperial violence, that a strong case could be made for his radical modernity.

It goes without saying that the boundaries of modernism are much less rigid than they once were. Paul Saint-Amour finds a splendid metaphor for this expanded sense of the modern in his recent book on war anxiety (where he writes about popular fiction as well as canonical figures) when he writes that "modernism" as a literary marker "has stopped playing bouncer and started playing host" (42). For Saint-Amour, this inclusiveness helps to explain why "'Modernist studies has become a strong field—populous, varied, generative, self-reflexive" (41). More specifically, surely it does not dilute the meaning of modernism to point out the modernity of Wells's kind of writing when it comes to war in particular, given that war as a subject—above most others, and second only to romantic love—has literally millennia of literary conventions behind it, all tending toward verbal mystification.

And so the cool, factual, eye-witness or correspondent style of a novella like *The War of the Worlds* perhaps intentionally recalls the newspapers to which it alludes (by name), but its reportage mode also anticipates to a remarkable degree a style of war writing that would prove invaluable for describing the real-world crises of the twentieth century: episodic, externalizing, quasi-objective, documentary. Here, to anticipate the end of the period associated with modernism, we might think of Tamiki Hara's autobiographical account of the dropping of the atomic bomb on his native Hiroshima in "Summer Flower" (1945), a story all the more harrowing for its almost automatized, unemotional exteriority as it describes a sequence of scenes, some outright nightmarish but all of them bizarre, as the narrator walks around the city in the aftermath of the blast: "I have to keep a record of this, I said to myself" (41). Or, returning to fiction, we might think of Albert Camus's Second World War occupation allegory, *The Plague* (1947), which is so insistent on the pseudo-objectivity of the documentary style that the identity of the "true" author is withheld for most of the novel:

> It is time for Dr Bernard Rieux to admit that he is its author. But before describing the last events, he would like at least to justify his role and to point out that he has tried to adopt the tone of an objective witness ... Being called upon to bear witness in the event of a sort of crime, he maintained a certain reserve, as a well-intentioned witness should. (232)

Cyril Connolly wrote on the eve of war in *Enemies of Promise* (1938) that modern writing could be divided into the "mandarin" and the "journalistic." He considered the last major representative of the "mandarin" to have been Woolf, but he had no doubt (and had some concerns) that the "journalistic" was the more distinctively modern mode (73). To make a case for Wells's modernity is to wonder how far the history of modernism and violence is connected to the contemporary emergence of the mass-market daily newspaper; indeed, Norris's *Writing War in the Twentieth Century* finds in modernist aesthetics' "hard, dry, concrete, objective, spare, crafted, disciplined language" as strong a debt to journalism as to the austere aestheticism of precursors like Flaubert (21).

But another reason why Wells is a relevant figure for thinking about the relationship between modernism and violence is that he shares with those contemporaries we think of as early modernists both his narrative framing devices and their concerns with civilization and violence. The dissolution of the cordon around modernism has made it possible to see how much common ground there is between writers like Conrad and Wells. To take an extreme example, *The Island of Dr Moreau* (1896), is closer to being a grotesque little shocker than many of Wells's writings, with its vivisected human/nonhuman hybrid monstrosities, but the ideas in circulation there make it retrospectively obvious how much of *Heart of Darkness* was written out of 1890s culture. The proto-fascist and self-deifying Dr. Moreau and Kurtz are metropolitan geniuses brought down by their lack of restraint, and in a passage wholly consonant with Conrad's understanding of civilization—and that of their contemporary Freud, for that matter—Dr. Moreau explains that his violent surgical work of rendering nonhuman animals closer to human is continuous with the social construction of the human in everyday life: "Very much, indeed, of what we call moral education is such an artificial modification and perversion of instinct; pugnacity is trained into courageous self-sacrifice, and suppressed sexuality into religious emotion" (79). And, as in Conrad (and, again, Freud), so-called civilization is a flimsy affair: after Moreau's death, the animal people are soon "reverting, and reverting very rapidly" to their former animal habits (141); back in England, Wells's narrator is troubled by the sense that "presently the degradation of the Islanders will be played over again on a larger scale" (149). Violence is both what creates "civilization," as Wells's grisly vivisection metaphor suggests, and what endangers it.

Conrad dedicated *The Secret Agent* to Wells, but a good example of the specifically formal as well as thematic overlap between the two writers comes earlier, in the numerous points of comparison between *The Time Machine* (1895) and *Heart of Darkness*, novellas that share not only their epistemologically wrong-footing use of narrative framing but their powerfully *fin-de-siècle* pessimism, set in a brutal colonial context. Whereas Wells's protagonist literally journeys through time to a moment at which the human being has divided into predator and prey in the year 802,701—and, in the supremely atmospheric later chapters, to a wholly post-human future—Marlow imagines that he has travelled backward through time by travelling through space. This view of civilization is what Wells's Time Traveller imagines in reverse, as if from the perspective of the future inhabitants of the earth: "What if in this interval the race had ... developed into something inhuman, unsympathetic, and overwhelmingly powerful? I might seem some old-world savage animal, only the more dreadful and disgusting for our common likeness—a foul creature to be incontinently slain" (22). Both texts share a sense of the relativity of temporal perspective: the West's perspective on Africa is destabilized by Marlow's imagining of how ancient Britain looked to a representative colonist from Rome, while Wells's Time Traveller asks his audience to "conceive the tale of London which a negro, fresh from Central Africa, would take back to his tribe!" (40).

As we have seen so far, then, the decades prior to the Great War offer unignorable examples of what will become the signature modes of modernist writing about violence. We find relativistic perspectives, heightened subjectivity, and an insistence on ironic and demystifying modes. In terms of thematic preoccupations, we find antimilitarism, skepticism, cultural pessimism, and a clear-eyed erosion of military-strategic oppositions of ally and enemy. To return, in closing, to the case for the importance of 1914, Fussell marvels at "the literary scene" at that moment:

> There was no *Waste Land*, with its rats' alleys, dull canals, and dead men who have lost their bones: it would take four years of trench warfare to bring these to consciousness. There was no *Ulysses*, no *Mauberley*, no *Cantos*, no Kafka, no Proust, no Waugh, no Auden, no Huxley, no Cummings, no *Women in Love* or *Lady Chatterley's Lover*. There was no "Valley of Ashes" in *The Great Gatsby*. One read Hardy and Kipling and Conrad and frequented worlds of traditional moral action delineated in traditional moral language. (23)

In retrospect, "traditional moral action delineated in traditional moral language" is an almost aggressively reductive view of Hardy, Kipling, and Conrad. No scholar of war can overstate her debts to Fussell, but one area in which his influence has proved misleading is in his overly dramatic insistence on a rupture between what is modern and what is not, leading to a highly selective and limited view of writers' implicitly naïve understandings of war prior to 1914. In Fussell's well-known words: "Irony is the attendant of hope, and the fuel of hope is innocence. One reason the Great War was more ironic than any other is that its beginning was more innocent" (18). But what Wells in *The War of the Worlds* called "the Great Disillusionment" was on its way long before August 1914 (3). Wells was writing in 1897, and his visions in that novel of postapocalyptic desolation prefigure the iconic wastelands of Eliot and all the many battlescapes to come in the twentieth century: "the countless ruins of shattered and gutted houses and blasted and blackened trees ... Never before in the history of warfare had destruction been so indiscriminate and so universal" (54).

Wars to come

The next chapter looks at the ways in which modernist writers used the First World War as an opportunity "to criticize the social system & show it at work, at its most intense," as Woolf wrote of *Mrs Dalloway* (*Diary 2* 248). When modernists write about the war, they are writing about all the areas of public and private experience that the war touched, and this chapter describes how critics have placed modernist writings about war in the contexts of far-reaching inquiries into areas such as gender, embodiment, and grief.

Chapter 3 considers writers' engagements with different forms of public violence, outside the sanction of the state, which have also been associated with the historical background of modernism, such as the insurgency, the terrorist outrage, and the conspiracy. This chapter focuses on two canonical phenomena: the anarchist panic, which finds its fullest expression in the novel, and the Independence struggle in Ireland from the Easter Rising in 1916 to the establishment of the Free State in 1922, where the best-known literary engagements are in poetry and drama. As critics continue to demonstrate, modernist writers showed some sympathy toward acts of symbolic and spectacular insurgency as rhetorical parallels to their own projects; however, this chapter also addresses the ways in which modernist irony undermines the mystique of "meaningful" violence.

Chapter 4 returns to war to address the ways in which modernism engaged overseas wars in the 1930s. The Spanish Civil War is especially important here, eliciting as it does major responses from writers such as Auden, Ernest Hemingway, George Orwell—and, in a more indirect way, Woolf, whose famous pacifist treatise *Three Guineas* (1938) is in part a product of that same conflict. War-watchers outside Spain also relevant for thinking about war in relation to a second generation of modern writers include Isherwood in Germany (*Goodbye to Berlin* [1939]); Evelyn Waugh in Abyssinia (*Scoop* [1938]), and the poet William Empson, caught up in the Sino-Japanese War, the war which also elicited the work that gives this chapter its title, Auden and Isherwood's *Journey to a War* (1939). This chapter emphasizes definitions of modernism in relation to debates about periodization (this is the era of "late" modernism) and changing styles of modernism in the era of the documentary movement.

Chapter 5 focuses on the renascent modernism of the Second World War, when the rehabilitation of modernist difficulty was indicated by the emergence of important work by both ageing high modernist writers (such as Woolf's *Between the Acts* [1941], Eliot's *Four Quartets* [1943], and Pound's *Pisan Cantos* [1948]) and those writers of the following generation most influenced by them (such as Henry Green and Elizabeth Bowen). The chapter focuses on two aspects of these second-wave modernisms: first, how they represent the war; second, how their understandings of this present war explicitly recall the traumas of the First World War and its aftermath, when high modernist images of the broken city take on, in this Second World War, a retroactively prophetic quality in the era of aerial bombing.

With catastrophe from the skies still in mind, my final pages consider a world-ending war that never literally happened but that has important consequences for thinking about modernism. This brief closing chapter sketches out the arguments that have been made, since the end of the Cold War, about the relationships between modernism and the first nuclear age when modernism was canonized and disseminated as the privileged exemplar of cultural production in the Cold War's "West." In Fredric Jameson's most uncompromising but influential view, all "modernism" is late modernism and a product of the Cold War. It was not simply that Cold War late modernism comprised belated formalist experiments from mid-century writers, but also, retroactively, the modernism of the 1910s and 1920s created in the process of its institutionalization at a time when the most useful modernism was an apolitical one. The decades since the end of the Cold War have rendered this concept of modernism untenable—as attested by this present book and the series of which it is a part.

2

Modernism and the Great War

Mr Britling was in a phase of imaginative release. Such a release was one of the first effects of the war upon many educated minds. Things that had seemed solid forever were visibly in flux; things that had seemed stone were alive. Every boundary, every government, was seen for the provisional thing it was.

H. G. WELLS, *Mr Britling Sees It Through* (197–8)

Described by Bernard Bergonzi as in its time "the most celebrated novel to describe reactions to the war on the Home Front," *Mr Britling Sees it Through* (1916) recounts the outbreak of war and the early wartime period (*Heroes' Twilight* 129). The novel's perspective is that of a Wells-like figure, for Mr Britling is a married (but romantically unfaithful—a surprising autobiographical addition) author of books with mass appeal and a progressive tone. This self-mocking, chatty novel, now little read, has the usual charm of Wells's realist Edwardian novels, but its idea that the war has suddenly put established values and boundaries up for grabs among "many educated minds" speaks more surprisingly to the relationship between modernism and war on which many later commentators wrote. It is by investigating this idea of a link between the war and the felt dissolution of old ideas that we might come close to approaching Wyndham Lewis's claim in *Blasting and Bombardiering* that the war in which he served was somehow "like" modernism. I have already discussed the long-standing critical sense of the First World War as a modernist point of origin, and this chapter turns to the ways in which critics have identified central high modernist problems with the First World War. The Great War brings into view problems of selfhood, psychology, and trauma; embodiment and emotion; the unsettling of traditional ideas about gender; problems of representation and linguistic crisis. This chapter surveys ways in which the war raised the social, cultural, and philosophical problems that proved to be among the concerns of the modernisms of the 1910s and 1920s, and describes how they continue to serve as lasting points of emphasis in modernist studies.

What these lines from Wells suggest, above all, is how widely contemporaries shared Lewis's sense of the war, in a line I quoted earlier, as akin to the break between "B.C. and A.D." Indeed, it would be hard to overstate the prevalence across the whole of the modernist period of the feeling that the First World War had ruptured historical continuity by unsettling what had once been taken for granted. Vincent Sherry describes the break with characteristic eloquence when he writes that the war "draws a line through time, dividing the nineteenth from the twentieth centuries" ("Literary Modernism" 113). In all such discussions, it is has become virtually obligatory to quote the charismatic passage from Walter Benjamin's essay "The Storyteller" (1936) on the silencing effects of war experiences that seemed to fall outside of all prior, prewar, frames of reference:

> Was it not noticeable at the end of the war that men returned from the battlefield grown silent—not richer, but poorer in communicable experience? What ten years later was poured out in the flood of war books was anything but experience that goes from mouth to mouth. And there was nothing remarkable about that. For never has experience been contradicted more thoroughly than strategic experience by tactical warfare, economic experience by inflation, bodily experience by mechanical warfare, moral experience by those in power. A generation that had gone to school on a horse-drawn streetcar now stood under the open sky in a countryside in which nothing remained unchanged but the clouds, and beneath these clouds, in a field of force of destructive torrents and explosions, was the tiny, fragile human body. (84)

Nothing in prewar culture appeared to have prepared people for the First World War, and, for Benjamin, the gap between what was known of old and what was actually lived during and immediately after the war was impassable and literally unspeakable. Everything was new, from a violent awakening to the fragility of the body confronted by the machine to the incomprehensible economic conditions of the 1920s.

What has proved critically significant here is that war is much more than an event, or series of events, taking place within contained spaces of battle, and the temporality of which will be contained by historians within a particular range of dates from the opening declaration of war to the cessation of hostilities. Rather, Benjamin is suggesting that the implications of the First World War radiated outward to touch all other areas of civilian or post-combatant life for years afterward, an insight that has been pursued by many subsequent commentators as they consider the range of discredited and emergent values and attitudes that modernist writing used the Great War to explore. This chapter asks, then, what new areas for scrutiny did the war make available to modernist writers? When modernists wrote about the Great War, what *else* were they writing about?

Modernism and the crisis of cultural authority

Sarah Cole writes in *At the Violet Hour* that literature "has always offered an exemplary forum for making violence knowable, showing how it can be simultaneously the crucible for a culture's highest values (in war, especially) and a force radically to undermine those ideals" (3–4). For obvious reasons, in both modernist writing and modernist studies at large the emphasis has fallen on the specifically *undermining* effect of violence on dominant cultural ideals, and the potentially confirmatory effect of war for British culture's values was either tacitly or actively denied. So prevalent is the modernist-instilled sense of prewar Britain as somehow deserving of its brutal awakening that it takes some historical effort to remind ourselves that things could have worked out quite differently. As George Orwell would later point out, amid what he considered all the

British self-flagellation about Versailles in the interwar years, the writers and intellectuals of the post-1918 period never seemed even to have asked themselves what would have happened if the nakedly expansionist, reactionary, and militaristic Germany of 1914 had actually won the First World War ("Looking Back" 253). And so the critical emphasis has fallen not on the First World War as a test of the values of prewar Britain relative to, for example, those it purported to be contesting in the war with Germany, but as the event that in both its prosecution and its conclusion proved these values to be fraudulent, inadequate, or hypocritical.

But, bracing as ever, D. H. Lawrence offered in *Lady Chatterley's Lover* (1928) a critique of prewar values that nonetheless refused to cast postwar modernism as a triumphant emancipation from the values of the implicitly benighted prewar past. On the contrary, Lawrence felt that the modernist present was nursing its own replacement falsities and illusions to replace those that the war had exploded. "Ours is essentially a tragic age," he wrote in the novel's famous opening, "so we refuse to take it tragically" (3). The publication of this, Lawrence's final novel, coincided with the famous "war books boom" of the late 1920s, and might usefully be seen in that context, given how effectively it identifies the rippling effects of war on the environments and attitudes of both combatants and civilians. When the novel opens, the diffident Scottish aristocrat Constance Chatterley has married an officer home on leave in 1917, and must deal with the aftermath of his later military service when after their honeymoon he is "shipped over to England again six months later, more or less in bits" (3). The novel casts Clifford Chatterley's smart, cynical, up-to-date conversation and writing as a soulless modernism that Lawrence wants us to understand less as a salutary critique of the old false values than as a symptom of the damage that the war has inflicted upon him. Clifford Chatterley has "been so much hurt that something inside him had perished, some of his feelings had gone" (4). Thus, he carries into peacetime the brittle, sardonic orientation that Modris Eksteins identified both with modernism and with wartime's "bitter and black" sense of humor (202). In what remains the most influential account of British literature and culture in the Great War, Paul Fussell argued that the war itself was a "satire of circumstance," and the famous argument around which *The Great War and Modern Memory* is built is that "there seems to be one dominating form of modern understanding; that it is essentially ironic; and that it originates largely in the application of mind and memory to the events of the Great War" (35). If Clifford Chatterley is criticized for that dark, ironic, disillusioned sensibility—in diagrammatic contrast to the unguarded erotic sincerity of his wife and her temporary-officer-turned-gamekeeper lover—Lawrence's own narrative voice participates in the same bitter irony that it also casts as a pathological symptom of war trauma. For example, there is not much difference between Clifford Chatterley's scathing view that "everything was a little ridiculous, or very ridiculous: certainly everything connected with authority, whether it were in the army or the government or the universities, was ridiculous to a degree.... Sir Geoffrey, Clifford's father, was intensely ridiculous" and the verdict of Lawrence's own third-person narrator on the same "ridiculous" patriarch: "Sir Geoffrey stood for England and Lloyd George as his forebears had stood for England and St George: and he never knew there was a difference" (9–10). This mockery of Sir Geoffrey's knee-jerk patriotism reminds us that Lawrence had been among the war's victims without having fought in it; he had come to feel persecuted by the suspicions directed by English neighbors at him and his German wife, as well as feeling vindictively singled out when wartime security regulations cast his works as prejudicial to national morale. The effects of the war on individual modern lives could obviously be more or less direct—an important idea for contemporary studies of modernism and the Great War as they trace the impact of war on civilian consciousness—and if Lawrence damns Clifford's postwar cynicism he also identifies with it to some extent.

The intimacy with which many civilian modernists such as Lawrence experienced the depredations of a war in which they could not fight finds illuminating expression in perhaps the least prestigious and, until recently, critically neglected of modern literary forms, the short story. At its oblique best, the small scale of the short story tends to privilege the private and personal aspects of war experience, making a virtue of the seeming inconsequentiality of a form that has never had to live up to the higher expectations made of drama, the novel, or (especially where war is concerned) poetry. As Ann-Marie Einhaus argues in her corrective recuperation of the period's magazine fiction, *The Short Story and the First World War* (2013), the short story has been an almost entirely neglected form in studies of First World War literature, despite its tremendous popularity during the war itself and within a literary culture in which magazine publication continued to thrive. Einhaus shows that, as with more canonical forms of war representation, the short story represents a very wide spectrum of political meaning, from the tub-thumping and propagandistic to the opaque, resistant, and inquiring. On the latter end of this spectrum, one of Lawrence's closest literary friends, the short story writer Katherine Mansfield, had an unusually strong investment in what the war meant for civilians, and, like Lawrence, she often presents the war as a form of cultural betrayal or failure on the part of authority.

Particularly for a female civilian, Mansfield had seen the war at close range when in the spring of 1915 she tricked her way into a restricted military zone near Dijon to visit her lover, French poet Francis Carco. The event is fictionalized in her best-known "war" story, "An Indiscreet Journey" – which is also, incidentally, a story of special historical interest because it includes one of the earliest literary descriptions of a victim of gassing, his red eyes weeping in his white face. Worse, later that year she lost her brother Leslie Heron ("Chummie") Beauchamp to the war, when he was killed in October in the course of a grenade demonstration in France—the official military incident report has recently been reproduced in a special issue of *Katherine Mansfield Studies* devoted to the importance of the First World War for thinking about her brief career (Mitchell 34). Mansfield's lacerating sense of loss is all over her journals of this time: "Yes, though he [Leslie] is lying in the middle of a little wood in France and I am still walking upright and feeling the sun and the wind from the sea, I am just as much dead as he is" (89). This grief finds expression in many of her short stories of the early 1920s, which even by the standards of the time are populated to a remarkable extent by dead bodies and those who mourn them.

Many critics have noted the prevalence of the dead body in modernist writing. Most recently, Elizabeth Outka has found in the postwar influenza pandemic that killed up to one hundred million people worldwide "the shadowed twin to the war, a disaster as unprecedented in its casualties and in its suffering" (938); in the autumn of 1919, she writes, "dead bodies were somehow everywhere in Britain, in America, and across the globe" (937), and the scale of the catastrophe helps to explain the prevalence in modernist writing of limbo states between life and death. David Sherman's *In a Strange Room* (2014) argues also for the significance of the corpse for thinking about modernism, both in and all around the Great War, and suggests that it offered modernists a new way of approaching notions of duty where other forms of social obligation had failed. The corpse imposes upon us what Sherman's subtitle calls "mortal obligations": implicitly the material remains of the human being make demands upon the living—demands for recognition, grief, and burial, for instance—and disruptively become "a site of ideological recalcitrance and disorientation, a vestigial thing only awkwardly available for modern processes of rationalization, secularization, marketizations, governmental regulation, and so on" (5). Similarly, the Great War is not the main topic of Ariela Freedman's *Death, Men, and Modernism* (2003), which argues that the figure of the dead young man had distinctive cultural meanings independent of the Great War. Nonetheless, the impact of the war is clearly present in her claim that in "the early twentieth century tragedy wears a male face. The face of the disaster is the face of a dead young man: with a cap and uniform, he is a soldier; with a crown of thorns he is a God. He is the culmination of masculinity, and at the same time, the sign of its decline" (3). In this vestigially religious culture, a dead young man conflates the crucified Christ and the fallen soldier.

But even by modernist standards, and even conceding Freedman's point about the widespread cultural prevalence of "the quintessentially modern figure of the young dead man" (3), there are an unusual number of bodies in Mansfield's post-1918 stories. Many of her most characteristic stories center on the premature death of young men, whether or not these stories are actually "about" the war. In "Life of Ma Parker," for example, a charwoman and the widow of a dead baker is reckoning with the imminent loss to lung disease of her beloved grandson. Both male figures, husband and grandson, have been symbolically asphyxiated in the course of everyday life, and, given the insistence of metaphors of choking and drowning (in gas, in mud) in trench writing, it requires no great ingenuity to see that Mansfield, whose tuberculosis would kill her in her thirties, is implying a parallel between the lung-diseased men of "Life of Ma Parker" and the soldiers, "coughing like hags" and "guttering, choking, drowning" in Wilfred Owen's "Dulce et Decorum Est" (29). We likewise find a reflection of the difficulty of national mourning in Mansfield's "The Daughters of the Late Colonel," which, despite its title, is not a story about the recent war but recounts the struggles of two middle-aged spinsters in the days following the death of their domineering elderly father, a retired colonial officer.

Reading as a war story another work with no manifest war content, Christine Darrohn has identified Mansfield's painful wartime loss as a source for one of her best-known short stories, "The Garden Party," first published in 1922, and set in her native New Zealand long before the First World War: "a story that depends on a man's violent death even as it erases the traces of injury from his body" (514). The story both reflects Leslie Beauchamp's sudden death and supplies narrative consolation for the unbearable physical horror of losing a brother to a grenade. At first sight, "The Garden Party" little resembles a war story: it is a coming-of-age narrative focalized through Laura, for whom adolescence in her upper-middle-class colonial world means both learning the social rules governing ladylike behavior and coming to terms with herself as a sexual creature. At the heart of this juxtaposition of the social and the sexual is Laura's encounter at the end of the story with the corpse of a young carter from her village who has been killed outside the gates of Laura's insulated home. Unlike the rest of her family, Laura does not apprehend yet that the social distance between classes trumps geographical proximity among the residents of the village, and so she tries unsuccessfully to cancel the garden party on the grounds that the dead carter and his family are, Laura thinks, "nearly neighbours" ("The Garden Party" 291). At the end of the story she visits the carter's family to pay her respects with a basket of leftovers from the party, and raptures ensue over the exquisite dead man, "so remote, so peaceful ... wonderful, beautiful," whose lack of visible injury presents a redemptive contrast to such ravaged human forms as that of Mansfield's grenade-killed brother (296). Mansfield is writing about the war without actually writing about the war, and in writing about the war is writing about the impossibility of mourning it adequately in a culture that lacks the psychological resources to acknowledge the magnitude of its losses.

This oblique form of reference has increasingly become a vital aspect of studies of First World War literature. I have already mentioned how Booth's *Postcards from the Trenches* finds modernism registering the war by repeatedly creating the sense that someone or something is missing, as when Booth links "the modernist fiction and the war memorials that pointed toward corpses buried elsewhere," an argument that makes modernism a kind of empty tomb analogous to Sir Edwin Lutyens's famous Cenotaph in Whitehall (33). Mansfield's fiction offers especially good illustrations of Booth's point about incomplete displacement of the war, and not least because we know from Mansfield's expressed views on what it meant to be a writer in the aftermath of the Great War that this obliquity of reference was purposeful and self-conscious. For example, in a frequently cited letter to her husband, the literary editor John Middleton Murry, Mansfield proposed that, irrespective of the subject of writers' work, the war imposes upon her generation a new moral imperative to remember the war.

> It's not in the least a question of material or style or plot. I can only think in terms like "a change of heart." I cant [sic] imagine how after the war these men can pick up the old threads as tho' it had never been. Speaking to *you* Id [sic] say we have died and live again. How can that be the same life? It doesn't mean that Life is the less precious or that the "common things of light and day" are gone. They are not gone, they are intensified, they are illumined. Now we know ourselves for what we are. In a way its [sic] a tragic knowledge. Its [sic] as though, even while we live again we face death. But *through Life*: thats [sic] the point. We see death in life as we see death in a flower that is fresh unfolded. (*Letters* 97)

Mansfield imagines postwar life as something close to a resurrection of sensibility and advocates a simultaneously aesthetic and moral melancholia: a refusal on the writer's part to put the past behind her means that the material world attains a new beauty through an awareness of its vulnerability and perishability. Freud made a similar point in his contemporary essay "On Transience," where he recalls a prewar trip to the countryside with a melancholy friend, "a young but already famous poet," since identified as Rainer Maria Rilke (305). The poet grieves at the thought that the beauty around them is "fated to extinction, that it would vanish when winter came, like all human beauty and all the beauty and splendour that men have created or may create" (305). In an attempt to console both the prewar poet, and implicitly the grieving wartime reader, Freud sets out to argue that beauty is not negated but enhanced by our knowledge of its transience, and that our anticipatory grief for what we know to be ephemeral only intensifies its claim on our attention and love. "We see death in life as we see death in a flower that is fresh unfolded," as Mansfield put it. Like Mansfield, Freud linked this sensibility to the war, which "robbed us of very much that we had loved, and showed us how ephemeral were many things that we had regarded as changeless" (307). "When once the mourning is over," he hoped in closing, "it will be found that our high opinion of the riches of civilization has lost nothing from our discovery of their fragility" (307).

Women modernists and the "old men"

To speak of 1920s modernism in terms of a postwar change of sensibility—Mansfield's "a change of heart"—is necessarily vague, and it should also be said that at other times Mansfield writes more explicitly than this about the aftermath of the war. Published in the same year as "The Garden Party," her story "The Fly" is explicitly about failed postwar mourning because the main character seems not really to recognize even after years have passed what his loss means for him. The story takes place in the postwar office of a prosperous businessman referred to only as "the Boss." It is six years since the Boss lost to the war his only son, and (a more painful loss for him, it is implied) his heir and successor. The story opens with a visit to the Boss's office from its previous occupant, Woodifield, whose advancing dementia implies from the outset Mansfield's concern with failures of memory. Like the Boss, Woodifield has also lost his son in the war, and describes how his wife and daughters have recently paid a visit to the war cemetery on the continent, "all as neat as a garden," where both men's sons lie buried (345). (Organized trips to the war graves had become an established industry by the early 1920s.) Woodifield's inability to focus on the actual loss this visit represents—his comments meander inconsequently around relative trivia about the cost of jam in the boarding houses—implies a warning to the Boss about managing grief: Woodifield has ceased to feel pain over his son's death not because he has mourned it successfully but rather because his powers of cognition are increasingly so impaired that his bereavement is only intermittently available to his consciousness. Upon his visitor's departure, the boss returns to his planned activity; as usual, he has set aside time in his day specifically to mourn his dead son—mourn inadequately and not wholly sincerely, the story implies. But again he is interrupted and distracted, this time by a fly drowning in the inkpot on his desk. Retrieving the fly only to keep splashing ink on him repeatedly until, exhausted, the fly can no longer find the energy to keep cleaning itself, the boss kills the fly and is overcome by an unnameable "grinding feeling of wretchedness" that suggests a parallel between the fly drowning in ink and a son dying by attrition in the muddy trenches (348). The unspoken link between the two is made more explicit by the pompous and unfeeling language of the armchair general in which the boss addresses the struggling fly: "a plucky little devil, thought the boss, and he felt a real admiration for the fly's courage. That was the way to tackle things; that was the right spirit. Never say die" (347).

This is a story about unacknowledged guilt and the boss's harrowing complicity in the authoritarian forces that killed his own son; it is, once again, the modernist story Samuel Hynes describes when he writes of an older generation of men accused of murdering their sons, as in Wilfred Owen's famous "The Parable of the Old Man and the Young," in which God tells Abraham to sacrifice the ram in lieu of the bound Isaac, "But the old man would not so, but slew his son, / And half the seed of Europe, one by one" (61). Confirming Hynes's argument, this rhetorical figure cuts across the work of trench writers and modernists. No less a figure than Eliot had put it to use in "Gerontion," a poem he had considered using as a prologue to (again, no less than) *The Waste Land*:

> Here I am, an old man in a dry month,
> Being read to by a boy, waiting for rain.
> I was neither at the hot gates
> Nor fought in the warm rain
> Nor knee deep in the salt marsh, heaving a cutlass,
> Bitten by flies, fought. (29)

He was not at Thermopylae ("the hot gates") when the Greeks fought the Persians; more to the purpose, he was not in the First World War either. A generation is missing in this poem: there are merely guilty and decayed old men and the boys who read to them. The young men are like "the loitering heirs of City directors" in *The Waste Land*, who, "[d]eparted, have left no addresses" (60).

As Hynes explains, this narrative of generational betrayal was useful for modernists in sanctioning their break with the past by denouncing the values held by the older generation: the war was the fault of the fathers and, deploying the vicarious logic of war whereby all members of a particular group are undifferentiated enemies, now all the fathers are to blame. It is not surprising that women writers such as Mansfield should have understood the war in literally patriarchal terms, and the view that traditional expectations about the masculine role bore culpable responsibility for the war and its destructive consequences is most obvious in the novels written by feminist modernists. Since the 1980s, the volume of work on women's responses to the First World War has proved formidable both in quantity and quality. To the extent that it is possible to identify a starting point, Sandra Gilbert's 1983 essay "Soldier's Heart" proved extremely influential, as did the 1987 collection *Behind the Lines: Gender and the Two World Wars* by Margaret Higonnet; the long line of notable works in this area includes Nosheen Khan's *Women's Poetry of the First World War* (1988), Claire Tylee's *The Great War and Women's Consciousness* (1990), Sharon Ouditt's *Fighting Forces, Writing Women* (1994), Suzanne Raitt's and Trudi Tate's *Women's Fiction and the Great War* (1997), Angela K. Smith's *Women's Writing of the First World War* (2000), Debra Rae Cohen's *Remapping the Home Front* (2002), and Jane Potter's *Boys in Khaki, Girls in Print* (2005). If this catalog implies homogeneity—it is probably a given that any emphasis on women writers will disproportionately represent middle and upper-middle-class women—some of these volumes nonetheless foreground "the *differences* among women" (both the phrase and the emphasis are from Raitt and Tate 3).

It would be relatively difficult to derive a feminist case against war from, for example, Willa Cather, awarded the Pulitzer Prize in 1923 for *One of Ours*, in which the masculine heroics and homosocial camaraderie of the Great War save Claude Wheeler from the miseries of his marriage to his frigid wife back in Nebraska. In contrast, former suffragette and radical journalist Rebecca West placed an unhappy marriage at the heart of *The Return of the Soldier* (1918) in order to diagnose the continuities between the pressures of the male role in peacetime and at war. West is a somewhat intermittent presence in modernist studies, despite her involvements in some of the major modernist projects; for example, her short story "Indissoluble Matrimony" appeared in Wyndham Lewis's 1914 issue of *BLAST* alongside the opening of the novel that became Ford Madox Ford's *The Good Soldier* (1915). But even as the rest of her fiction goes largely unread, the extremely Ford-like novella *The Return of the Soldier* continues to command critical attention. The protagonist, or ostensible protagonist, since he is seen not from within but only from the perspective of the women around him, is the soldier, landowner, businessman, officer, and country gentleman Chris Baldry, who is a victim throughout the novel of the expectations attendant on his public roles. Narrated by his war-haunted cousin Jenny, the novel opens with Chris's repatriation from France in 1916 as a war casualty suffering from such severe shell shock that he has blotted from his memory the past fifteen years of his life. These missing years of adult responsibility include not only his wartime career but also marriage to his elegant but (from Jenny's point of view) vacuous wife Kitty, and Chris believes himself instead to be the acknowledged lover of Margaret. Fifteen years prior to the mid-war present, Margaret had been the great love of Chris's adolescence but is now a shabby and downtrodden working-class housewife in a neighboring suburb. What is extremely characteristic of this novel among works by feminist modernists is the extent to which it interprets the war not as a shockingly unique tragedy but as a catastrophe made possible and explicable by its broader ideological context. West insists that the exit from Edenic boyhood that culminates in Chris's comprehensive breakdown in the trenches happens not when he enlists in 1914, but years earlier, when his apoplectic father forces upon Chris unwanted responsibilities to his family business; this fall from happiness is compounded in the years leading up to the war by the economic demands of his wife's concern for appearances and the need to keep up their lavish country estate. West's point here seems to be that the war that requires Chris's presence as a British officer is merely one among many coercive and interlocking masculine roles. Indeed, these forces become coercive to the point of fatality once the three women in his life—Chris's wife, his lover, Margaret, and his cousin, narrator Jenny—resolve that Chris must be cured of the amnesia that renders him physically safe as well as socially incapacitated, on the grounds that were he to be left in his blissful amnesia, and so unfit to be returned to the Front, "he would not be quite a man" (88). And so, as a man, he must be returned as a soldier—and the novel's title clearly has multiple meanings that link home and battlefield, whereby the soldier returns home in order to be returned to war—in order to fulfill his masculine destiny by dying in France.

There are obvious similarities with Virginia Woolf's *Jacob's Room* (1922), another diagnosis of the lethal continuities among a range of traditional upper-class masculine roles; Woolf would later declare these continuities explicitly in her feminist-pacifist treatise *Three Guineas* (1938), where she traces both more forensically and polemically the links between violence and the socialization of young men. *Jacob's Room* takes the form of fictional modernist biography or experimental *Bildungsroman*; as in *The Return of the Soldier*, the male character to which the title refers is not the novel's center of consciousness, for Woolf's protagonist, like Chris Baldry, is largely a construction of the admiring women characters through whose eyes we see him. We follow the upbringing of the unambiguously named Jacob Flanders through the various male and protectively homosocial environments (which implicitly have taught Jacob his unreflectively casual misogyny) and rites of passage from a pampered childhood as the center of his widowed mother's world to his career at Cambridge, his Greek travel, and his sowing of gentlemanly wild oats in London before embarking upon a career that never gets the chance to come to fruition because it is forestalled by a war in which he must play his part. (This theatrical metaphor is the novel's own: "Poor Jacob," one character says: "They're going to make you act in their play" [81].)

Michael André Bernstein's powerful arguments against narrative foreshadowing, which sees the present only "as the harbinger of an already determined future" (1), are obviously relevant to the representation of the Great War. The psychological utility of foreshadowing is obvious: a way of responding to the unanticipated magnitude of the war, it also raises the question of whether or not, in fact, it could and should have been foreseen. In Joseph Roth's *The Radetzky March* (1932) as in Robert Musil's *The Man Without Qualities* (1930–43), the reader waits for the war to break out, and life among the elite of prewar Austro-Hungary is shadowed by our knowledge of their culture's imminent annihilation. *The Man Without Qualities* is famously unfinished in this respect and others—hence Bernstein's use of this novel as an exemplary refusal of foreshadowing—whereas war is inevitable for Roth's characters, who are "still unaware that each of them, without exception, would have an assignation with Death within a couple of years," and cannot "hear the machinery of the great hidden mills that were already beginning to grind out the Great War" (98). At no point does Woolf's narrator undertake Roth's kind of intervention, but, even so, all the sequential phases in the life of Jacob Flanders are tending toward his death in the Great War. The seeming incomprehensibility of Jacob's death is strikingly shown—only then to be shown up—by the novel's final chapter when Jacob's mother and best friend stand in his empty room wondering what to do with his old shoes. Rather, Woolf's point is that there is nothing at all incomprehensible about Jacob's death: it is exactly what he was born and reared for.

Mansfield had criticized the novel Woolf wrote immediately prior to this one for being worse than old-fashioned in its disengagement from the events taking place during its composition. Although published after the war, *Night and Day* (1919) had turned instead to the suffragette and socialist ferment of the prewar period.

> My private opinion is that it is a lie in the soul. The war has never been, that is what its message is. I don't want G. forbid mobilisation and the violation of Belgium, but the novel cant [sic] just leave the war out. There *must* have been a change of heart. It is really fearful to me the "settling down" of human beings. I feel in the profoundest sense that nothing can ever be the same [and that] as artists we are traitors if we feel otherwise: we have to take it into account. (*Letters* 82)

It is striking, then, that Woolf's novels from 1922 onward are all touched by war, and all powerfully concerned with, if not "a change of heart" as such, the need for the radical kind of cultural change that could put an end to the naturalizing of warfare. For example, *Jacob's Room* is clearly not about Jacob as a traditionally conceived character but as a canvas on which cultural beliefs and values get sketched out, often in a faintly satirical way, as in the tendency of all around him to idealize Jacob, who is not, in himself, anything more than an unremarkable product of upper-class masculine privilege. That these values are either obsolescent or deserve to be obsolete is obvious in this novel and then later in a more sorrowful way in

To the Lighthouse (1927), when the novel's shocking middle section kills off not only the angel in the house, Mrs. Ramsay, but her natural successor, the beautiful and ultra-feminine daughter Prue, along with scholarly Andrew, heir to his father's no less gendered academic expectations.

Posttraumatic modernism

As far as thinking about war is concerned, perhaps no major modernist writer has benefited more than Woolf from the historicist turn in modernist studies. At least since the publication of Alex Zwerdling's *Virginia Woolf and the Real World* (1986), scholarship on Woolf has been highly attentive to what Nancy Topping Bazin and Jane Hamovit Lauter describe as "Woolf's keen sensitivity to war" in the title of an essay published in Mark Hussey's groundbreaking collection *Virginia Woolf and War* (1991), and Karen Levenback extends this work in *Virginia Woolf and the Great War* (1999). Consequently, it has become almost impossible to ignore how recurrent a presence the Great War is in Woolf's fiction, even though the war is always happening or has happened or is about to happen somewhere outside her novels' ostensible fields of vision. Indeed, *Mrs Dalloway* (1925), her next novel after *Jacob's Room*, is explicitly about the ways in which the war has infiltrated each corner of everyday life. If the shell-shocked and death-bound veteran Septimus represents the most obvious casualty of a war that refuses to recede into history, characters touched by the war range from the history tutor Miss Kilman, who is sliding into lonely poverty, having lost her job for refusing to endorse the demonizing anti-German propaganda, to the character who has simply turned over one morning in wartime and died on the grounds that he had "had enough" (13). "The war was over, thank heaven, over," Mrs. Dalloway thinks, but even her own train of thought goes on to correct that relieved, but clearly over-insistent, claim:

> For it was the middle of June. The War was over, except for someone like Mrs Foxcroft at the Embassy last night eating her heart out because that nice boy was killed and now the old Manor House must go to a cousin; or Lady Bexborough who

opened a bazaar, they said, with the telegram in her hand, John, her favourite, killed; but it was over; thank Heaven—over. (4)

Of course the war will never be over for these bereaved mothers, even if the national stiff upper lip ("opened a bazaar ... with the telegram in her hand") dictates that their grief will remain private and self-consuming ("eating her heart out") rather than a disruptive public acknowledgement of the war's cost. Furthermore, public attempts at commemoration are fatally compromised by the militarism of their conduct, as we learn when Peter Walsh watches a band of young reservists on their way to lay a wreath at the Cenotaph:

> I can't keep up with them, Peter Walsh thought, as they marched up Whitehall, and sure enough, on they marched, past him, past everyone, in their steady way, as if one will worked legs and arms uniformly, and life, with its varieties, its irreticences, had been laid under a pavement of monuments and wreaths and drugged into a stiff yet staring corpse by discipline. (66)

These boys are described as if they were as unconscious as the dead men whose loss they mark, and, just to drive the point home about the emptiness of pro forma efforts at official collective mourning, Woolf seems almost to have conflated the two main focal points for national commemoration, the Cenotaph ("marched up Whitehall") and the Tomb of the Unknown Warrior in Westminster Abbey ("laid under a pavement of monuments and wreaths"). As Tammy Clewell points out in a persuasive discussion of Woolf and mourning, official forms of mourning tend in Woolf's fiction to betray the dead they purport to grieve by attempting to master it too conclusively (25–55).

And it is the same kind of official repression that helps to kill Septimus, who, years after the war, is unable even to grieve for his lost friend and former officer Evans because normal human feeling has been killed in the war:

> But when Evans (Rezia, who had only seen him once, called him "a quiet man," a sturdy red-haired man, undemonstrative in the company of women), when Evans was killed, just before the Armistice, in Italy, Septimus, far from showing any emotion or recognising that here was the end of a friendship, congratulated

himself upon feeling very little and very reasonably. The War had taught him. (112–13)

With its ironic echo of the Harley Street doctor's smug belief in the normalizing and health-giving virtues of "a sense of proportion," Septimus's self-congratulation on "feeling very little and very reasonably" reveals what Woolf sees as the essentially pathological qualities of the culture of the stiff upper lip, since this numbing that comes with Evans's death is obviously a symptom of Septimus's embryonic shell shock. In Ernest Hemingway's contemporary short story "Soldier's Home" (1925), we see the same kind of affectlessness in Harold Krebs, Midwestern veteran, and a story in which the belatedness of his demobilization serves to allegorize the belatedness of trauma, for by the time he gets back to Kansas all the war stories have already been told and no one is interested in his experience. Like Woolf's Septimus, urged to take up cricket in order to reinsert himself into normative male pursuits, Hemingway's Krebs can muster none of the enthusiasm he is expected to show about a return to such conventionally masculine interests as women and work.

Woolf goes further, though, by drawing so strong a parallel between what happens to Septimus and to civilians in a culture of emotional repression. It has always been acknowledged that Clarissa and Septimus are doubled characters as they crisscross central London together on that June day in 1923: "I adumbrate here a study of insanity & suicide: the world seen by the sane & the insane side by side," Woolf had written in her diary (*Diary 2* 207). But shell-shocked Septimus finds a double even less likely than the Tory hostess Clarissa when, as if in passing, we learn a little about Lady Bradshaw, wife of the ultra-successful, ultra-establishment Harley Street specialist who fails, with fatal consequences, to comprehend Septimus's predicament:

> Fifteen years ago she had gone under. It was nothing you could put your finger on; there had been no scene, no snap; only the slow sinking, water-logged, of her will into his. Sweet was her smile, swift her submission; dinner in Harley Street, numbering eight or nine courses, feeding ten or fifteen guests of the professional classes, was smooth and urbane. Only as the evening wore on a very slight dullness, or uneasiness perhaps, a

nervous twitch, fumble, stumble and confusion indicated, what it was really painful to believe—that the poor lady lied. (131)

This metaphor of "sinking" and "going under" is more usually used of Septimus: "I went under the sea," he thinks (89). And what are those strange symptoms that betray Lady Bradshaw's unhappiness with her flawlessly establishment life? What could be more like shell-shock symptoms than her telltale "nervous twitch, fumble, stumble and confusion"?

Many historians and literary critics have remarked upon the way in which the psychological trauma of war found somatic expression in the bodies of combat veterans. "War neurosis, like neurosis in peacetime, was a flight from an intolerable, destructive reality through illness," as historian Eric Leed put it in his influential 1979 work *No Man's Land: Combat and Identity in World War I* (164). Elaine Showalter amplifies this point in *The Female Malady* (1987), where she explains how an illness axiomatically associated with women ("hysteria") jeopardized conventional notions of masculinity when, in the Great War, it suddenly made an appearance in those men charged with saving the nation itself (167–94). The implications of trauma for reading modernism have been discussed in depth more recently by a range of critics including Carl Krockel in *War Trauma and English Modernism* (2011), Wyatt Bonikowski in *Shell Shock and the Modernist Imagination* (2013), and Trevor Dodman in *Shellshock, Memory, and the Novel in the Wake of World War I* (2015).

If war serves as the socially approved testing ground for masculinity—which is why, Woolf argues in *Three Guineas*, it is so inordinately hard to eradicate from human life—the test is liable to be "failed" in modernist works. In some ways, then, Ford Madox Ford's classic impressionist novel *The Good Soldier* (1915) was virtually prophetic in its concern with the intersection of trauma, disempowerment, and the erosion of traditional ideals. Notwithstanding the title, however, this is not a novel "about" the Great War: it was conceived beforehand and its insistence upon domestic tragedies happening on the devastating date of August 4—the date on which the war actually broke out in 1914—was merely an accident; material from the novel, then still titled "The Saddest Story," was published in *BLAST* the summer before the war. Ford had volunteered in 1915 and held a commission in the Welch

Regiment, an experience that he would put to use in his important four-novel sequence *Parade's End*, along with the experiments he had made with the representation of trauma as temporal disruption in *The Good Soldier*. In *Parade's End* the Christian Tory gentleman landowner Christopher Tietjens watches both on and off the battlefield the devastating effects of war, and the psychological trauma war generates is replicated formally in the novel by radical time shifts and passages of demandingly subjective narration similar to those Ford had developed immediately prior to the war.

Another prescient aspect of *The Good Soldier* was Ford's attentiveness to the incomplete nature of survival, a dominant trope in the fiction of the early postwar years, and the basis of important work on modernism and grief. Among these works are Patricia Rae's valuable collection *Modernism and Mourning* (2007) and Clewell's *Modernism, Mourning, Postmodernism* (2009), both of which emphasize the interplay and antagonism between experimental writing (and the forms of defamiliarization it enables) and other commemorative practices such as monuments and rituals. Jay Winter has described the war's aftermath in an almost literally haunting way when he writes that "Europeans imagined the postwar world as composed of survivors perched on a mountain of corpses" (17). Here, we might think of *The Waste Land*, with its crowds "undone" by death flowing over London Bridge (55), an image recalling the opening lines of war poet Charles Hamilton Sorley's harrowing sonnet: "When you see millions of the mouthless dead / Across your dreams in pale battalions go" (191). The feeling of living-dead nightmare was already scripted, though, if we think back to the hallucinatory aftermath of the alien invasion in Wells's *The War of the Worlds*:

> I go to London and see the busy multitudes in Fleet Street and the Strand, and it comes across my mind that they are but the ghosts of the past, haunting the streets that I have seen silent and wretched, going to and fro, phantasms in a dead city, the mockery of life in a galvanized body. (186)

In an influential reading Maud Ellmann saw in Eliot's discursive writing as well as his poetry a haunting by "the voices of the dead" (101), and there is a critical tradition going back decades of emphasizing the death at Gallipoli of French medical officer Jean Verdenal (the dedicatee of 1917's *Prufrock and Other Observations*) as a devastating event in Eliot's life. *The Waste Land* would probably always have been read as in some sense a war poem because of its use of the same tropes conjured up in the passage from Wells: automaton-like and ghostly urban citizens surviving in the surreal half-life of the aftermath of a disaster. Less than a year into the Great War, Freud was already suggesting in "Thoughts for the Times on War and Death" that "we are unable to maintain our former attitude towards death, and have not yet found a new one" (292). Working out a way to apprehend mass slaughter is among modernism's projects in the 1920s.

That said, there is potentially a cost to focusing on the social meanings and effects of war rather than its bodily realities, and studies of war typically have to deal with the tension between how literature deals with war as discourse and how to think about war as bodily violence. In emphasizing the latter, scholars are often indebted to Elaine Scarry's discussion of the soldier in *The Body in Pain* (1985), and particularly her point that "while the central activity of war is injuring and the central goal in war is to out-injure the opponent, the fact of injuring tends to be absent from strategic and political descriptions of war" (12). A disembodied modernism runs the risk of repeating the military strategist's gesture, which may be why Margot Norris, whose reservations about modernist war writing as a form of non-representation are among the strongest, turns to German avant-garde poet, and war veteran, August Stramm to indicate that formal experiment need not entail abstraction. She quotes "Haidekampf":

Blut
Und
Bluten
Blut
Und
Bluten Bluten. (Norris 56)

"Blood / And / Bleeding / Blood / And / Bleeding bleeding." The reader feels the ebbing of the wounded soldier's life as drops of blood begin to puddle at the foot of the poem. This extremely visceral performance—so visceral that the poem can be apprehended in either language—shows that the historic separation of soldier or "trench" writing from modernist experiment is more a British construction than a fact about the relationship between abstraction and historical representation when it comes to war. As far as the novel is concerned, we could reach a similar conclusion from the former soldier Louis-Ferdinand Céline's nihilist classic *Journey to the End of the Night* (1932) in which the deeply reluctant soldier Bardamu, Céline's semi-autobiographical surrogate, hears of the aftermath of war as his family "joyfully gamboling on the lawns of a new summer ... while three feet under papa, that's me, dripping with worms and infinitely more disgusting than ten pounds of turds on the Fourteenth of July, will be rotting stupendously with all my deluded flesh" (56).

As the example of Céline also suggests, the literary afterlife of the Great War extended into the 1930s. By then, the meaning of the war as a tragic waste was largely established, and became a kind of touchstone as writers thought about new and emergent conflicts. "We were all C.O.'s [conscientious objectors] in the Great War," Woolf wrote in 1937 as she attempted a memoir of her writer nephew Julian Bell, killed in the Spanish Civil War: "What made him do it?" she asked: "I have never known anyone of my generation have that feeling about a war" (28). Of course that is not literally true, given that not all modernists were civilians, let alone pacifists, and given that most British writers would have agreed with Lewis when he wrote in the "War Number" of *BLAST* (1915), the magazine's second and final issue, that "it appears to us humanly desirable that Germany should win no war against France or England" (5). What Woolf's claim does reflect, though, is the powerful, and decidedly interwar, remembering of the Great War as something no intellectual ("we") could conceivably have supported. This view of the unthinkability of the Great War became ever more the received wisdom as the interwar period went on.

Meanwhile, and all the way through the 1930s, the Great War continued to produce major modernist works. In 1937, under Eliot's editorial watch, Faber & Faber published David Jones's *In Parenthesis*, perhaps the most overtly experimental of works by British veterans, a work operating amphibiously between poetry and the novel. The book recounts the Front Line experiences of Private John Ball in the months between December 1915 and the catastrophic summer of 1916, experiences corresponding to Jones's own time as a soldier with the Royal Welch Fusiliers in the run up to Mametz Wood, where he was injured and sent back to Britain. In his "Note of Introduction" to *In Parenthesis* Eliot claims Jones explicitly for modernism as one of the "Men of 1914":

> David Jones is a representative of the same literary generation as Joyce and Pound and myself, if four men born between 1882 and 1895 can be regarded as of the same literary generation. David Jones is the youngest, and the tardiest to publish. The lives of all of us were altered by that War, but David Jones is the only one to have fought in it. (viii)

Eliot's obvious agenda here is to ward off the idea that Jones is somehow derivative of an earlier "generation" of modernists—Eliot's own—given the echoes of high modernism that imply Jones's indebtedness to the writers who began their career in the 1910s. As Eliot had for *The Waste Land*, Jones provides his own explanatory endnotes, for example, and there is also the marked layering of mythic and literary pasts upon the wartime present, a tendency that led Fussell to argue that *In Parenthesis* "is a deeply conservative work which uses the past not, as it often pretends to do, to shame the present, bur really to ennoble it" (147); still, despite its "defects," he felt that the book "remains in many ways a masterpiece impervious to criticism" (154).

Certainly this must be the only serious modern war book in which going up the line for the first time is given so much dignity, when "some certain, malignant opposing, brought intelligibility and effectiveness to the used formulae of command; the liturgy of their going-up assumed a primitive creativeness, an apostolic actuality" (28). And yet if this kind of theological abstraction can feel overworked, *In Parenthesis* can be grotesquely effective when it turns to the materiality of war experience, as here, when for the first time Private Ball sees soldiers clearing out their trench:

> Appear more Lazarus figures, where water gleamed between dilapidated breastworks, blue slime coated, ladling with wooden ladles; rising, bending, at their trench dredging. They speak low. Cold gurgling followed their labours. They lift things, and a bundle-thing out; its shapelessness sags. From this muck-raking are singular stenches, long decay leavened; compounding this clay, with that more precious, patient of baptism; chemical-corrupted

once-bodies. They've served him barbarously—poor Johnny—you wouldn't desire him, you wouldn't know him for any other. Not you who knew him by fire-light nor any of you cold-earth watchers, nor searchers under the flares.

Each night freshly degraded like traitor-corpse, where his heavies flog and violate; each day unfathoms yesterday unkindness; dung-making Holy Ghost temples.

They bright-whiten all this sepulchre with powdered chloride of lime. It's a perfectly sanitary war. (43)

Jones's endnote informs us that around the middle of this passage ("They've served ... flares") he is alluding to Eddeva Pulchra, the beautiful wife of Edward the Confessor, and the Norman poet Wace, but also has "various 'traditional song' associations" in mind (197). That does not seem the most penetrating feature of the passage compared to the ways in which it describes the profanation of the human, and the disjunction between selves made meaningful by love, religion, or the state and the pure horror of Johnny's rotting corpse.

London-born Jones identified substantially with his Welsh ancestry, and for other non-metropolitan-minded modernists, too, the Great War belatedly takes its place in a historically dense elegiac perspective. For example, the Scottish writer Lewis Grassic Gibbon commenced his trilogy *A Scots Quair* with the novel *Sunset Song* (1932), set in an isolated community in the North East of Scotland in the years around the First World War. Stylistically an extremely unusual novel, *Sunset Song* is narrated in a kind of synthetic vernacular that replicates the voice of the protagonist Chris and her community, with no commentary from an external perspective: this form of narrative underscores in powerful ways the limits of what could be known about Britain's London-based political culture from within an isolated community on the eve of war. The community cannot possibly know that the war will be its destruction as the men of the village get caught up in and destroyed by an event whose causes and prosecution could not be more remote from their rural lives. Retrospective (and implicitly less sheltered) knowledge on the reader's part means we know more than they can. Thus, what would otherwise be a lightheartedly satirical presentation of a prewar rural by-election, in which the parliamentary candidates canvass the votes from a community in which everyone knows that neither candidate will ever set foot after the General Election, takes on a more sinister quality as we realize that in 1914 the decisions these strangers take at Westminster will determine the lives and deaths of the remote constituents whose votes they court.

What the reader does not see coming, though, are the different ways in which the war will devastate the community: not only are men killed in combat, men such as the socialist Chae Strachan who is increasingly deceived by the hate-the-Hun propaganda of the press, and Long Rob of the Mill, ruined by his conscientious objection to the war and broken into submission; most shockingly of all, we learn that Chris's husband Ewan, a volunteer shamed into enlisting by his own neighbors calling him a coward, has died not in combat like the others but because he has been shot at dawn by his own side as a deserter when he comes to believe that this war was essentially not his to fight. "*Country and King?*" asks his angry widow, Chris Tavendale: "*What have they to do with my Ewan, what was the King to him, what their damned country?*" (238–9). (Historically, the British shot 306 servicemen for crimes of this kind during the Great War; after decades of activism from their descendants, these executed men received a posthumous pardon in 2006 [Hochschild 371].) At the end of *Sunset Song*, the warmongering old minister whose sermons report "how the German beasts now boiled the corpses of their own dead men and fed the leavings to pigs" is finally replaced, but all too late, by a more adequate spokesman for the broken community (221). This incoming minister preaches his first sermon not on a scriptural text but on the damning anti-imperial line Tacitus put into the mouth of Calgacus, the Caledonian freedom fighter who unsuccessfully fought the Roman occupiers: "*They have made a desert and they call it peace*" (255).

Through the modernist works of the 1920s and 1930s, then, the First World War increasingly took on the qualities of an ending. If the modernism of 1914 had been assertive, even aggressive, in its readiness to set fire to the values of the past, what we find afterward is a writing that is more inward and elegiac in its treatment of the world that was lost, even as it insists upon the inadequacy, or even the falsity, of its values. "Shall we lay the blame on the war?" Woolf asked in *A Room of One's Own* (1929), wondering why it was no longer possible to write love poetry as the Victorians had:

> When the guns fired in August 1914, did the faces of men and women show so plain in each other's eyes that romance was killed? Certainly it was a shock (to women in particular with their illusions about education, and so on) to see the faces of our rulers in the light of the shell-fire. So ugly they looked—German, English, French—so stupid. But lay the blame where one will, on whom one will, the illusion which inspired Tennyson and Christina Rossetti to sing so passionately about the coming of their loves is far rarer now than then. One has only to read, to look, to listen, to remember. But why say "blame"? Why, if it was an illusion, not praise the catastrophe, whatever it was, that destroyed illusion and put truth in its place? (17)

Why not praise it, indeed? But of course she never does. Like Eliot's dispossessed Marie recalling sled rides with her cousin, the Archduke, or Septimus Warren Smith his adoration of Miss Isabel Pole walking in the square in her green dress, postwar modernism shows the difficulty, and not simply the necessity, of giving up on what has been lost.

3

Modernism and political violence

> *So I remember all of those whose death*
> *Is necessary condition of the season's setting forth*
> W. H. AUDEN, "It Was Easter as I Walked in the Public Gardens" (8)

> *Did that play of mine send out*
> *Certain men the English shot?*
> W. B. YEATS, "The Man and the Echo" (393)

Although the losses that Auden's poem goes on to catalog are essentially personal, perhaps it was inevitable that the language of sacrifice he used when he described the deaths of other people as a "necessary condition of the season's setting forth" should have been so readily available in a period marked by two world wars. That *they died for us* remains a traditional formula and rationale for remembering the war dead, because it gives meaning to the losses of war by imagining them as the price paid for the continued sovereign life of a national community or the survival of its culture. But, as critics have shown, right across the period we associate with modernism there were other important historical moments at which death could be cast as a "necessary condition of the season's setting forth," beyond those losses sanctioned or transfigured by the full force of a state at war. As important for modernism are revolutionary acts *against* the governing state, which partook at least as much as—at times even more than—those committed at the state's behest in the moralized and aestheticized narratives of martyrdom and sacrifice that Sarah Cole terms "enchanted violence" (*At the Violet Hour* 40), and which Pericles Lewis sees as a "redemptive violence" that shaped modernism (148). As Robert Buch writes in *The Pathos of the Real* (2010), a study of violence and continental modernism, the twentieth century cast up many for whom violence was "not just a necessary means for the transformation that is to be achieved; it functions like a token of the faith and commitment to the cause of radical change" (14). Thus, political violence needs to be understood as more than merely a regrettable means to a particular end because the very willingness to die or kill has such powerfully symbolic qualities that it is practically aestheticized even before the poets get near it.

When he has his speaker anchor his thoughts on the price paid by the dead to a walk in "the public gardens" at "Easter," Auden recalls the traditional meanings of Easter as sacrificial crucifixion and triumphant resurrection. He also evokes what in the context of Anglophone modernism is among the most important instances of transfigured violence, the Easter Rising in Dublin in 1916, the event that provoked the famous lines from Yeats quoted in my other epigraph. Public gardens are, axiomatically, a site of national remembrance in that they are where a nation's great men (and women in principle, but mostly men) are monumentalized in statuary. The imperial implications of this use of public space would be picked up much later by Philip Larkin in "Homage to a Government," his poem about Britain's postimperial military retrenchment: "The statues will be standing in the same / Tree-muffled squares, and look nearly the same," but the young will have inherited a diminished nation: "Our children will not know it's a different country" (171). Here, as for Auden, the public garden is the public sphere and an official archive of the nation's historical engagements with violence.

This chapter considers modernism's engagements with political violence outside the mandate of the state, for we find in modernism a powerful interest in acts of bloody and sacrificial violence that recall war and yet are driven by motives that are not licensed by the state, but typically find its firepower directed strenuously against them. This is the world of the revolutionary, insurgent, or terrorist outrage, and it is not surprising to find that since 9/11, and throughout the era of the war on terror, modernist critics have been especially attuned to literary representations of this brutal version of the spectacular, finding in the writing of the early twentieth century a persistent concern with how it feels to live in an age marked by the tactical use of unpredictable violence.

In *Plotting Terror* (2001), Margaret Scanlan finds among a number of modern novelists a tendency to see the terrorist as a double and rival; she argues that narratives of terrorism allow writers to examine or test the power of literature to effect change in the world (2). It is certainly striking how often writers use terrorism to talk about art, and a satisfyingly complex early example of this apprehended similarity between the author and the assassin would be Henry James's *The Princess Casamassima* (1886) in which the qualities that draw the sensitive Hyacinth Robinson into the revolutionary critique of social injustice are those that might otherwise have made him a writer ("in secret, he wrote," we learn, on meeting him for the first time as an adult: "he had a dream of literary distinction" [112]). And then, ironically, it proves to be his connoisseur's fear of destroying beauty that leaves him incapable of committing the violent act for which he has been enlisted.

Many critics have identified rhetorical similarities between the political outrage and the modernist author's own will to shock. Writing of "the inherent modernity of terrorism" (2), Deaglán Ó Donghaile cites Max Nordau's identification of the "unhealthy impulses" of the *dynamitard* and the political anarchist with those of the proto-modernist "degenerate" author (5). Likewise Alex Houen's *Terrorism and Modern Literature* (2002) includes, alongside chapters on the representation of literal acts of terrorism, discussions of the "allegorical assaults" of the experimental periodical (93). Houen writes of "an avant-gardisme that becomes increasingly terroristic"' (92), while Ó Donghaile argues that at the turn of the century "the act of dynamiting became translated into modernism's militant blasts against the inert weight of the literary establishment" (10), proposing a direct continuity between the two. If these analogies between writing and terrorism feel on the face of it overblown—even distasteful—it is demonstrably true that the self-descriptions of the avant-garde were given to recalling the violence of their times. Not that they were always being entirely serious: here, we might think of Joseph Conrad's punning use of "outrage" in his author's note to his dynamite novel *The Secret Agent* (1907), in which he declared himself innocent of any desire "to commit a gratuitous outrage on the feelings of mankind" (252), or his presumably joking claim that he felt at times like "an extreme revolutionist" while writing the novel (251).

Potentially revolutionary civil unrest assailed cities as different as Chicago and St. Petersburg as the nineteenth century turned into the twentieth. This politically febrile period saw a US President assassinated in Buffalo and a French President in Lyon; other assassinations took out an Austrian empress, an Italian king, a Spanish prime minister, and Ireland's Chief Secretary. Revolutionary socialists assassinated the liberalizing Tsar Alexander II in 1881, and while his conservative successor survived an assassination plot, the next Tsar would be the last. The Russian Revolution obviously has its own important and complex story to tell about the relationship between modernism and politics given that, as Martin Puchner points out, communism and the avant-garde "shared a common root" (95), and yet modernism's flowering in Russia would be cut artificially short by the more instrumental and ideological view of the arts that led to the privileging of socialist realism and the disavowal of futurism's claims to be the art of the revolution.

Back in the Anglo-American world, revolutionary terror was merely interesting for the most part, producing volumes of sensationalist plots. Correcting "America's amnesia concerning its history of terrorist violence" in a book published two years after 9/11, Jeffory Clymer describes how turn-of-the century novelists such as James, William Dean Howells, and Jack London engaged with contemporary terrorism either in real life or in their fiction (3). In Britain, volumes of terrorist plots were published at this time, from the pot-boiling adventure of Robert Louis and Fanny Van de Grift Stevenson's stories in *The Dynamiter* (1885) to G. K. Chesterton's philosophical and self-reflexive *The Man Who Was Thursday* (1908), in which, although a work of conventional Edwardian realism in terms of its form, characters actively debate the relationship between literature and anarchy. Modernist fiction about terrorism, however, both deploys and destabilizes violence at the level of style.

"Bewilderment" and the modernist novel

Along with cinema, the novel is among the most important forms for the representation of political conspiracy, and, more than representation, for the dramatization and narrative embodiment of its disorientating effects. But the specifically *modernist* novel's interest in complicating how we know what we think we know lends itself especially well to the treatment of political conspiracies that, of necessity, rely on the creation of confusion and indirection about who, exactly, people really are and what they are setting out to accomplish. Reading novels such as James's *The Princess Casamassima* and Conrad's *The Secret Agent*, and *Under Western Eyes* (1911), it becomes impossible to separate the formal difficulties that the fiction presents from the secrecies and willed obscurities of the conspiracy and political double-dealing that form the thematic core of the spy novel. Or, as James put it in the preface to *The Princess Casamassima*, what is needed is "that bewilderment without which there would be no question of an issue or of the fact of suspense, prime implications in any story" (37).

In his influential *Postmodernist Fiction* (1987), Brian McHale distinguished between modernist and postmodernist fiction by linking the former with detective fiction and the latter with the spy novel. Modernism and detection are concerned with questions of knowledge ("epistemology"), whereas postmodernism and espionage are concerned with questions of being ("ontology") (McHale 9–10). The distinction is neat and illuminating: the experiments of modernist fiction typically bring into the foreground the ways in which consciousness obscures as well as accesses knowledge, while the collapsing of different levels of reality is unmistakably among the dominant features of both spy fiction, with its secret agents and double agents, and of the kind of postmodernist fiction in which the world of the text collides with the world of the reader. Nonetheless, McHale's binaries are obviously suggestive rather than definitive, and to ask why writers like James and Conrad should explicitly have engaged questions typically associated with spies and conspirators—and with "ontology," on McHale's definitions—is to start unpacking connections with modernism and violence that are politically more complicated than the binary constructions of war writing, where allegiances may be patriotic or (more canonically) antipatriotic but tend not to fluctuate in as unstable a way as we find in the novel of conspiracy.

To begin with the most celebrated and most studied modernist instance: given the traumatic opening of the twenty-first century, it is not surprising that there has been a massive surge of critical interest in Conrad's *The Secret Agent*. The editors of *Conrad in the*

Twenty-First Century (2005) describe how the critical reception of Conrad's fiction—in a phenomenon they trace all the way back to 1902—has been the history of claims for his timeliness. Conrad has always "been recognized as current, with something crucial to tell contemporaries about themselves and the world they live in"; but, even so, "since the beginning of the twenty-first century, things have taken a peculiarly Conradian turn," beginning with 9/11 and the almost instant invocation of *The Secret Agent* by commentators (Kaplan et al. xiii).

The Secret Agent is ostensibly historical in that it was inspired by a botched anarchist outrage in Greenwich Park in 1894, when the anarchist and would-be terrorist Martial Bourdin destroyed only himself when he set off his bomb, and the novel was published only as the shocking heyday of anarchist terrorism had started to fade. As Antony Taylor explains, what was most significant about the anarchy scare was the purity with which—like modernism, we might add—it "distilled many of the social fears of the fin de siècle period, and reflected prevalent anxieties about the collapse of the cultural and political certainties of the nineteenth century" (46). Yet, however historical it may have been even in its own time, *The Secret Agent* also feels creepily modern in ending not with those late Victorian anarchists whose moment seemed already to have passed, but with the figure of the suicide bomber, the key figure for terrorism in our own time. This is the threatening trajectory into the future that Sarah Cole finds in the novel as she surveys the fictions of "dynamite violence" at the opening of the modernist era, and the implications of this trajectory are discussed at length by Peter Mallios in an essay that describes the forms of press attention *The Secret Agent* received in the aftermath of 9/11 (155–72). In fact, Mallios proposes that what feels most contemporary about *The Secret Agent* is its understanding of terrorism as necessarily intertwined with modern media dissemination, reliant as terrorism is on the possibility of projecting threat swiftly and across very long distances in the form of shocking "news" [155].)

In one sense, we could consider modernism and terrorism as fundamentally at odds: if terrorism speaks with literally visceral force of the assailant's hatred and anger, modernism speaks obliquely and indirectly. But both are concerned with the revolutionary—and Puchner's *Poetry of the Revolution: Marx, Manifestos, and the Avant-Gardes* (2005) gives an especially comprehensive account of the relationship between political revolution and the modernist manifesto all the way up to the 1960s—and both are, after all, trying to say something. Unpacking the anarchist Bakunin's doctrine of "propaganda by the deed," Cole writes of politically inspired violence that "its defining feature is the idea that violence is a potent form of political expression": "Violence, in that sense, becomes its own kind of language, and a host of terminology is called upon to describe this relationship: acts of terrorism can be seen as statements of belief or creed, threats of future violence as messages written in bodies and blood" (*At the Violet Hour* 21). But Conrad foregrounds these questions of articulation as problems of unintelligibility in *The Secret Agent*, through, for example, the dead ends created by the circles Stevie endlessly sketches; these are purely self-contained and have no referent whatsoever. They are "comic variations on modernist geometric form," according to Adam Parkes, as if Stevie were an unwitting Vorticist draughtsman (123). This is one among many instances of *The Secret Agent*'s emphasis on the problem of meaningfulness and senselessness: it is precisely the problem Conrad explicitly raised in his preface when he mentioned the newspaper story out of which his own plot emerged: "a blood-stained inanity of so fatuous a kind that it was impossible to fathom its origin by any reasonable or even unreasonable process of thought. For perverse unreason has its own logical processes" (249).

This idea that what is irrational is fundamentally unassimilable proves to be the core of the anarchist act when Vladimir, the novel's foreign agent who forces lazy Verloc into the kind of action he would otherwise avoid, speculates on a suitably insane target: "what is one to say to an act of destructive ferocity so absurd as to be incomprehensible, inexplicable, almost unthinkable; in fact, mad?" (27). Vladimir settles on the Greenwich Observatory as a figure for scientific reason since, as he reluctantly and with dark comedy concedes, it is impossible to "throw a bomb into pure mathematics" (27). For Vladimir's purposes, the more meaningless the terrorist act appears—the harder to decipher—the more shocking and destabilizing, and thus effective, it might be. He is reversing the whole idea of terrorism as a means of expression, targeting symbolic or metonymic targets: the violent medium is now almost the entire message.

When Conrad writes about terror, then, he is writing about reading and readability. Among the causes of helpless Stevie's death is his excessive trust in the reliability of language, its referential relationship to real-world acts; he takes quite literally the anarchists' inflammatory metaphors, not realizing that these are clapped-out clichés of the kind Conrad himself mocks. Cliché is, after all, among the targets of *Under Western Eyes*, particularly through the risible humbug of the Bakunin-like revolutionary Peter Ivanovitch: "The admirable Russian woman! I receive most remarkable letters signed by women. So elevated in tone, so courageous, breathing such a noble ardour of service!" (86). Famously, the narrator of that novel, an English teacher of languages based in Geneva, describes the human capacity for speech as akin to the facility of a parrot (5), associates silence with "sincerity" (124), and quotes approvingly the view that "speech has been given to us for the purpose of concealing our thoughts" (185).

On the face of it, *Under Western Eyes* appears to be concerned with less complex structures of political violence than those from which *The Secret Agent* takes its wrong-footing plot. The uncompromising brutality of the Tsarist state elicits the insurgent violence of the revolutionaries, which is then countered by the repressive violence of a state driven by self-preservation. But like its precursor, *Under Western Eyes* took its inspiration from real events, the aborted Revolution of 1905 in Russia, at a time when both political assassination and brutal state repression were facts of ordinary life, although in the words of Conrad's 1920 foreword, subsequent events in Russia had now rendered it "already a sort of historical novel dealing with the past" (lxxxiii).

As Rebecca Beasley, Philip Ross Bullock, and Caroline Maclean have most recently described, the period associated with modernism saw a vogue for all things Russian among Anglophone watchers of culture, from Sergei Diaghilev's *Ballets Russes* and (thanks to the prolific translator Constance Garnett) Russia's nineteenth-century novelists to the esoteric wisdom of Pyotr Ouspensky. But all eyes were on Russia in 1917, when "one hundred and sixty millions of the world's most oppressed peoples suddenly achieved liberty," as American journalist John Reed dramatically described the Russian Revolution (x). Reed's *Ten Days that Shook the World* (1919) told the story of the October or Bolshevik Revolution in 1917 as he had witnessed it at first hand, in a work that remains a journalistic classic, albeit of an admittedly partisan kind ("my sympathies were not neutral" [xiii]). (Its first English publisher was the Communist Party of Great Britain.)

In contrast, Conrad's interest in the revolutionary foregrounds the ironies of failure. The protagonist of *Under Western Eyes*, Razumov, is the illegitimate son of an eminent member of the Tsarist establishment whose favor he seeks. Here, Conrad follows the presentation of Hyacinth Robinson in *The Princess Casamassima* in making illegitimacy stand for a kind of placelessness at the level of citizenship. The same is true of the revolutionary Maxim Tsiepherkin in Philip May's inexplicably forgotten political novel *Love, the Reward* (1885), set in Russia and published four years after the assassination of Tsar Alexander II. Maxim "shares the common fate of nations, in as much as the first period of his existence is much enveloped in mystery" (28), and like Razumov he is a St. Petersburg student in political disgrace. May's preface calls the novel "a sketch of the Russian people, and especially of those who are desirous of effecting some change in the government of their country," and, bravely in view of the date, offers one of the most sympathetic contemporary presentations of the so-called Nihilists ("the present generation ... condemns every liberal Russian politician, whose enemies call him a Nihilist" [iii]).

The most obvious difference between *Love, the Reward* and *Under Western Eyes* is the characteristic irony that gets Razumov unwillingly into politics, despite that among his main aims is avoiding negative attention from the authorities, when Razumov's taciturnity is catastrophically misread as silent support by radical fellow students. (Ironically enough, his solitary, sober, self-denying asceticism enhances this false perception of him as a potential hero of the revolution: he fits the idealized profile of the radical thinker and potential martyr in a way that the novel's undisciplined insurgents do not.) Razumov is interrupted at his studies one winter's night by his classmate Haldin, who, it transpires, has been responsible for the assassination of the repressive minister of state and ideologue Mr. de P ---. Whether he decides to betray Haldin or to assist him in his getaway from Russia, Razumov knows that, whatever he does, his own career is over, since even the more conservative possibility of surrendering Haldin to the authorities will leave him an object of lifelong suspicion—for why would Haldin have entrusted his life to him unless he had reason to believe that Razumov shared his political sympathies? After Razumov betrays Haldin, we pick up the story again in the Russian émigré community in liberal Geneva, and, in classic spy fiction style, Razumov's current political sympathies appear to those around him to be revolutionary, although they are initially obscure to the reader. Significantly, this part of the novel initially holds Razumov at a distance, because the narrative is pieced together by and filtered through the perspective of the elderly teacher of languages, who neither likes nor understands stories with "associations of bombs and gallows – a lurid, Russian colouring which made the complexion of my sympathy uncertain" (81).

The relationship of "uncertainty" as a feature of contemporary political life to "uncertainty" as a principle of modernist narrative form is finely explored in Parkes's *A Sense of Shock* (2011), which sets out to recover modernist impressionism from the long-standing critical tendency to see this narrative mode in unhistorical and purely phenomenological terms, "detached from the dynamic and sometimes volatile historical contexts in which its various manifestations took shape" (5). Like Houen, Parkes notes the common linguistic ground occupied by anarchist terror and the rhetoric surrounding literary modernism, but with the interesting difference that Parkes shows how the tags of lawlessness, belligerency, anarchy, and the incendiary were used by *commentators* on impressionism as far back as the 1860s and 1870s, long before that kind of rhetoric was claimed by literary modernists for themselves (Parkes 10–11). Conrad is among Parkes's strongest instances of the historicity of the connection between modernist impressionism and violence, and he reads his fiction in relation to the sensationalism shared by terrorists, the emergent mass media they exploited, and those impressionist styles in literary fiction that proved, Parkes writes, "peculiarly apposite" for conveying the shock of sudden violence (100). Time shifts, layering of narrators and points of view, and the recourse to what Ian Watt had famously called "delayed decoding" (270) all work to replicate the disorientations of terror—or, in Parkes's astute summary, "a typical Conrad tale works like an orchestrated sequence of increasingly powerful detonations or shocks" (100).

"There's no amendment to be got out of mankind except by terror and violence," the anarchist "Mr X" proposes in Conrad's short story "The Informer" (1906), often considered a precursor to *The Secret Agent*. (It includes, for example, the prototype of the nihilistic "Professor," the maker of detonators.) "You can imagine the effect of such a phrase out of such a man's mouth upon a person like myself, whose whole scheme of life had been based upon a suave and delicate discrimination of social and artistic values," responds the art-collector narrator to the assertion of the necessity of "terror and violence" (290). What happens, in fact, is that the anarchist and the aesthete prove to have much in common as specialists in what is "unappreciated by the vulgar" (287); instructively, the narrator is only introduced to Mr. X in the first place by a fellow connoisseur, "collector" of Mr. X, who is himself "an enlightened connoisseur of bronzes and china," as a particularly fine "specimen" of his terroristic type (288). Here as in *The Princess Casamassima* the terrorist plot intersects with discussions of high culture; the revolutionary politics of James's princess are plainly a form of dilettantism along the same lines as her collecting practices. The connection between violence and connoisseurship is deployed even in the Stevensons' *The Dynamiter* when a terrorist contemplates the "elegance" of wiping out cities by targeting their drainage systems to create typhoid epidemics, while choosing himself to retain the "more emphatic, more striking bomb": "I have something of the poet in my nature" (185).

When the narrator of "The Informer" proclaims "anarchists in general were simply inconceivable to me mentally, morally, logically, sentimentally, and even physically," that absurd final addition ("physically") confirms that he is protesting too much (306). Like Conrad, he is fascinated by the politically motivated violence from which he recoils. One reason for the fascination for a novelist is obvious: what this kind of violence allows Conrad to write about is the problem of literary character. Among all of Conrad's novels, those about terrorism are the ones that foreground most explicitly the opacity of other minds, and of other people's values, motives, and intentions. From the beginning to the end, Razumov's tragedy in *Under Western Eyes* is that in almost every character he encounters, regardless of their political orientation, he "inspires confidence": this term is used throughout with growing irony (15, 29, 36, 39, 126). Indeed, both the recurrence of "confidence" and its ironic ramifications reach the point where the word makes even Razumov himself laugh in bitter recognition "'I have the gift of inspiring confidence.' He heard himself laughing aloud" (156). All the other characters around him are able to project their own wishes on to his taciturn self. It is only when he and Natalia Haldin fall in love—an echo of the Kurtz–Marlow–Intended triangle in *Heart of Darkness* in which a woman who has been excluded from secrets the men share is then blamed for her ignorance—that his capacity for inspiring belief in the nobility of his soul is destroyed. And this happens not because anyone sees through him but only because Razumov destroys his own cover with a Dostoevsky-style confession in which he tells Natalia that she has made the same mistake as her brother: "you have done it in the same way, too, in which he ruined me: by forcing upon me your *confidence*" (252, emphasis added).

Razumov writes in his diary, "I begin to think there is something about me which people don't seem able to make out" (71). The illegibility of other people entails the unpredictability of other people, and what that means in *The Secret Agent*, most of all, is a radical severance of objectives and consequences right up until the final scene of the novel, precisely because people's knowledge of the motives of others is at best guesswork and more usually an instrumentalist expression of their own wishes. *The Secret Agent* ends with a shot—the cinematic vocabulary is hard to resist in discussing this novel, with implications Mark Wollaeger has described (38–70)—of a terrorist of obscure motives walking through London with a bomb in his pocket, ready to detonate. He is untouchable because the police cannot know if he really *will* kill them and himself by setting off his threatened bomb at the point of arrest: "What is effective is the belief those people have in my will to use the means. That's their impression. It is absolute. Therefore I am deadly" (54). The scene in which this potential suicide bomber walks unnoticed and unimpeded among the unknowing urban crowds capitalizes on the anxiety Houen identifies so well when he writes that "what was terrifying about dynamite-terrorism was not simply its propensity to kill. It was also its impersonal randomness, which revealed to people that they were *already living as potential statistics*, already living as anonymous figures in a crowd" (25). By the end of the novel, then, Conrad has ironically achieved the unsettling power to which the sinister paymaster Vladimir aspired but never actually achieved. Within the novel, we recall, the terrorist outrage amounts to no more than a grotesque oddity for the handful of people who read about it in a few sensationalizing paragraphs of the evening paper. Modernist irony makes nonsense of political commitment.

According to one character in *Under Western Eyes*, "women, children, and revolutionists hate irony, which is the negation of all saving instincts, of all faith, of all devotion, of all action" (197). Irony presumably is the preserve of men and of (male) novelists.

As these words perhaps suggest, *Under Western Eyes* is conservative in its political orientation. Revolutionary terrorism is, as Conrad's prefatory note to this novel has it, merely "senseless desperation provoked by senseless tyranny" (lxxxiv):

> These people are unable to see that all they can effect is merely a change of names. The oppressors and the oppressed are all Russians together; and the world is brought once more face to face with the truth of the saying that the tiger cannot change his stripes nor the leopard his spots. (lxxxv)

Most likely Conrad's counsel of despair is informed by his familial background, and by the suffering of his Polish parents when the Russian regime convicted his father for nationalist activism. Underlying this bluntly conservative assertion, though, is a more fundamentally modernistic nihilism whereby outcomes are absurd and senseless in ways none of the characters can anticipate.

Actions and consequences, objectives and outcomes, are fundamentally divorced from one another. This aspect of Conrad's fiction is most explicit in his novels about terrorism, political violence being above all about the relationship between radical action and would-be beneficial and achievable ends. Ultimately, it is the abysmal gulf that opens up between what is done with conscious intention and what is actually realized that gives *The Secret Agent* a nihilistic quality of its own. Lazy Verloc delegates his terrorist's task to his mentally impaired young brother-in-law Stevie, who trips on a tree root and is blown up; he is swiftly identified by a nametag his devoted sister has stitched into his coat to keep him from getting lost. And here unintended political outcomes find their domestic counterparts, for Stevie's sister Winnie has only married Verloc in the first place, and against her own romantic desires, to ensure what she believed would be a secure home for her troubled brother, beginning the chain of events that leads to Stevie's grotesque death. This is a world in which characters conceive of each other primarily as means to ends: how Verloc sees Stevie, how Winnie sees Verloc. Completing the domestic tragedy, Winnie's readiness to use her husband's seedy friend Ossipon is thwarted by Ossipon's use of her, leading to a suicide that is, in a final irony, the consequence of her fear of death.

Ireland's wars

Given how plot works in time, novels have special advantages in dramatizing these gaps between motives and acts, and between intended aims and actual consequences. Still, these gaps are an important feature of modernist writing about political violence more generally. As Michael Wood writes, "Yeats is a poet almost everyone associates with violence" (7), and the subject of Wood's analysis, "Nineteen Hundred and Nineteen," is full of bitter reflections on the disillusioning disparity between theory and practice: "We pieced our thought into philosophy, / And planned to bring the world under a rule, / Who are but weasels fighting in a hole" (233). In "Sixteen Dead Men," named for the ringleaders of the Easter Rising, the insurgency and the British response to it have destroyed other historical hopes:

> But who can talk of give and take,
> What should be and what not
> While those dead men are loitering there
> To stir the boiling pot? (205)

There was once, the poem proposes, a time when people could debate the relationship between England and Ireland even during war ("You say that we should still the land / Till Germany's overcome" [205]), but no rational conversation can be had now that the fact of martyrdom is present to "stir the ... pot"—a homely image of inflammatory intervention, here posthumously conducted by those who were killed by the British and whose deaths implicitly have not yet been avenged. As far as aims and consequences are concerned, this was not, to put it mildly, the outcome for which the English had hoped either. That pre-Civil War hopes of peace and justice for Ireland gave way to a squalid culture of reprisals also explains the dark symmetry of Sean O'Casey's best-known play, *Juno and the Paycock* (1924), which ends with Johnny, the son of the title character, being shot as an informant by the IRA, the play having opened with the discovery of the bullet-ridden body of a neighbor's son whom Johnny betrayed and who was believed to be, in a particularly grim pun, a "Die-hard" (6).

The violent situation in Ireland overlaps historically with the phenomenon of anarchist violence on which Conrad based *The Secret Agent*. The overlap is particularly obvious in the "Fenian" bombings that took place on the British mainland late in the century. For a number of critics, Oscar Wilde's first play *Vera, or the Nihilists* (1882), in which, as in *The Princess Casamassima*, the extravagantly melodramatic war between the protagonist's finer feelings and his or her violent political commitments are resolved only through suicide, is one example of how an interest in anarchism overlaps with liberationist insurgency in Ireland. Barbara Melchiori finds it "hardly surprising in view of the analogy with his Irish background" that Wilde "should have turned to "the Nihilists' fight for freedom" in this early play (151); Michael Newton argues that notwithstanding the fashionably exotic Russian setting, *Vera* essentially uses Russia as "a substitute for Ireland" (38) and as a way of thinking through domestic politics. Sos Eltis likewise argues that although Wilde may have been ambivalent about the bloody methods of the anarchists, his "lifelong sympathy with revolutionaries and their ideals embraced the cause of the Russian nihilists" (30).

But with Anglophone modernism specifically in mind, the climactic act of insurgency was the Easter Rising, when around a thousand Irish Republicans seized a number of public buildings in the middle of Dublin, most famously the General Post Office, on April 24, or Easter Monday, of 1916, and unilaterally declared an independent Irish Republic. Ineptly underwriting the narratives of martyrdom that always threatened to emerge around the event, the British executed by firing squad fifteen of the Rising's leaders in prison that May as part of a typically counterproductive overreaction. "As insurrections go, it was not a military success," Fran Brearton dryly writes: "Nevertheless, the execution of the rebels had a much greater imaginative impact in Ireland than the deaths of thousands in the Great War" (18). And so these men became martyrs, with their deaths a heroic symbolic origin for an independent Ireland. "O plain as plain can be," Yeats later wrote in the voice of poet-insurgent Patrick Pearse: "There's nothing but our own red blood / Can make a right Rose Tree" (206).

"This country is gone mad. Instead of counting their beads now they're countin' bullets," a character announces in O'Casey's *The Shadow of a Gunman* (1923), in a line that captures the ease with which the service of the nation can take the place of religious belief (39). As Benedict Anderson pointed out in his seminal *Imagined Communities* (1983), nationalism may be a modern phenomenon but it shares with traditional religion its ability to create followers willing to sacrifice their lives in its service (10). *The Shadow of a Gunman* is full of men and boys either declaiming or disclaiming their readiness to die for an independent Ireland, although, ironically, they all survive unscathed and it is only brave, innocent, and silly Minnie Powell who dies as collateral damage in a gunfight. Something similar happens in O'Casey's *The Plough and the Stars* (1926) in which the main victims of male politics are the apolitical Nora Clitheroe, her stillborn baby, and the staunch Unionist Bessie Burgess. As in Conrad, the victims of male political aspirations range from the merely unfortunate to the heavily ironic: women and children like Stevie and Winnie Verloc, Natalia Haldin, Nora Clitheroe, Bessie Burgess.

Any country as culturally Christian as Ireland would have had a ready-made language for sacrifice—the symbolism of both "Easter" and "Rising" could not be more obvious—and the considerable body of criticism dealing with the literature of the Easter Rising registers the strange sense it conveys of an event that had been written into existence long before it actually took place. In *Inventing Ireland* (1995), for instance, Declan Kiberd noted the "aura of the 1890s"—of aestheticism, symbolism, decadence—surrounding the Irish rebels: "Seeing themselves as martyrs for beauty, they aestheticized their sacrifice" (201). Kiberd quotes a poem by executed insurgent Joseph Plunkett, "The Little Black Rose [Ireland] Shall be Red at Last": "Praise God, if this my blood fulfils the doom / When you, dark rose, shall redden into bloom" (201). "Perhaps history is never so amenable to the workings of the imagination as before it actually happens," writes Brearton of the Easter Rising, "even if any amount of revision can be attempted afterwards" (34). So, did Yeats's and Lady Gregory's *Cathleen ni Houlihan* (1902) send out "certain men the English shot"? Wood calls it "a question that has been much quoted and brilliantly mocked" (187). He cites Northern Irish poet Paul Muldoon's deflationary alternative: "If Yeats had saved his pencil-lead / Would certain men have stayed in bed?" (189). But even Wood is somewhat ambivalent in his response. On the one hand, Yeats's question is "too directly causal to be taken literally"; on the other, he concedes that the play's aesthetic of sacrifice for sacrifice's sake was also part of the "moral climate in which they made their choices" (188).

But if their national literature at the turn of the century had given Irish insurgents a romantic and sacrificial language for their struggle, as Kiberd and Brearton argue, it had also supplied a mocking critique of it. In Oscar Wilde's would-be fairytale "The Nightingale and the Rose," a nightingale bleeds her heart out in an erotic moment of sacrificial ecstasy to turn a white rose red for the pining protagonist to give to his lover. Only then does this hardheaded young mistress decide that she prefers gifts more durable than a single red rose. So if there were prefabricated rhetorics for transfiguring sacrifice into art, Irish literature also had a recent history of treating that transfiguration ironically.

As a text debunking the allure of violence and the heroic young man, J. M. Synge's best-known work, *The Playboy of the Western World* (1907), could not be improved upon. Set in a remote Mayo community shortly after the Boer War, this deathlessly funny play shows all the women falling in love with Christy Mahon, who takes refuge in their village. The villagers are all too ready to assign Christy a heroic, and here specifically anti-English, backstory:

> **Philly:** Maybe he went fighting for the Boers, the like of the man beyond, was judged to be hanged, quartered, and drawn. Were you off east, young fellow, fighting bloody wars for Kruger and the freedom of the Boers? (105)

Christy opts for a more private form of treason as his personal myth when he claims that he has run away from home after murdering his own father. This parricidal story of insurgency against authority is no less acceptable to the people of Mayo, who bestow upon Christy all sorts of intoxicating qualities not otherwise evidenced in his looks and conversation. We learn when the "murdered" Mahon shows up in Act 2 that Christy is in fact less than a nobody in his own community, and, indeed, is a figure of ridicule: "the girls would stop their weeding if they seen him coming [up] the road to let a roar at him and call him the looney of Mahon's" (127), his bemused father recalls: "I never till this day confused that dribbling idiot with a likely man" (134). But for as long as the illusion lasts, hopeless Christy is a romantic hero in the eyes of the community, and, in a telling extrapolation from their faith in his murderous capacities, no less than a poet: "I've heard all times it's the poets are your like, fine fiery fellows with great rages when their temper's roused," says the heroine, Pegeen (109); she is left at the end of the play to lament the possibility of a forthcoming marriage not to the playboy, but to "a middling kind of scarecrow with *no savagery or fine words* in him at all" (139, emphasis added). "So obsessively are poetry and violence interwoven in the mental fabric of the Mayoites that the women seem incapable of describing poetry except in terms of violence, and unable to imagine violence except as a kind of poetry," writes Kiberd (169–70). This connection between poetry and violence would prove darkly prophetic on Synge's part, in light of the droll, brutal British officer whom Kiberd later quotes on the quashing of the Easter insurgency: "The Irish ought to be grateful to us. With a minimum of casualties to the civilian population, we have succeeded in removing some third-rate poets" (225). This intersection of poetry and violence is encoded neatly in the disenchanted nationalist Seumas Shields's punning description of Ireland as "a land of *bloody* poets" in O'Casey's *The Shadow of a Gunman* (5, emphasis added).

Surveying Irish writing about the First World War, Brearton notes how "the Rising's cultural legacy has, it appears, almost completely sidelined the legacy left by the Great War in the Republic of Ireland": "One perhaps slightly too easy view might be that the Easter Rising literature *is* Ireland's Great War literature" (15). One hundred fifty thousand Irish fought among the British forces in the Great War and around 35,000 were killed. If the execution of the men who led the Rising turned them from traitors to the British Empire into martyrs for a free Ireland, there was always going to be something potentially more awkward to simplify into any kind of myth about those who voluntarily fought with the British; in the absence of Irish conscription, they may have been fighting for the rights of other small nations such as Belgium (some additionally took the view that fighting abroad would expedite Home Rule for Ireland), or simply for any combination of the various and many reasons for which an Englishman, a Welshman, or a Scot might have chosen to fight. Eugene McNulty has described the way in which these bodies resist assimilation: "remaindered," he calls them. However, Keith Jeffery believes that the extent to which these men were written out of national memory has been overstated, and also that "a historiographical revolution" has taken place to correct the alleged "national amnesia" on this topic (*Ireland and the Great War* 1). Insofar as this elision happened at all at the time, Jeffery argues elsewhere, it happened only unsystematically and belatedly since the government of the Irish Free State continued to support forms of war commemoration well into the 1930s ("Writing Out of Opinions" 257).

Of course some Irish writers, and Yeats most canonically, wrote about both the Great War and the independence struggle. Perhaps as a result of the problems that loyalty entailed, "An Irish Airman Foresees His Death," his poem for his patroness Lady Gregory's son Robert, killed flying for the Royal Flying Corps in the final year of the war, is among the most strangely neutral of all Great War poems. In the poem, the airman is in all senses above earthly concerns: "Nor law, nor duty bade me fight, / Nor public men, nor cheering crowds, / A lonely impulse of delight / Drove to this tumult in the clouds" (152). Gregory becomes an aristocrat in all senses, and Brearton notes how the poem reinstates all the values the Great War "had apparently negated—individual heroism, the sense of tragedy, the prophetic capabilities of art" (57). Instead of the "passive suffering" that Yeats had identified with the unpoetic or antipoetic in his notorious dismissal of Owen ("not a theme for poetry"), the airman is triumphantly artistic and aristocratic in death.

Another able, if outside Ireland less canonical, modernist commentator on both Ireland's wars and the war in Europe was O'Casey, who contributed to the late-1920s war books boom with *The Silver Tassie* (1928). Examining the war from the perspective of working-class Irishmen in the trenches, the play shares the antiestablishment tone of many contemporary works, as evidenced at the start when a stage direction explains that Irish athlete Harry Heegan "has gone to the trenches as unthinkingly as he would go to the polling booth. He isn't naturally stupid; it is the stupidity of persons in high places that has stupefied him" (186). Although *The Silver Tassie* is more overtly modernistic than O'Casey's earlier work, in that between naturalistic home-front scenes there appears a hallucinatory, expressionistic second act set in a ruined monastery on the Front, and although it diminishes regional and national differences among working-class soldiers (the war scene sees the Irish characters suffering alongside soldiers from as far afield as London and the Lake District), in some ways it is continuous with his plays about the Easter Rising and the Civil War. This is particularly true of its concern with the humble victims as opposed to the heroes of conflict, reflecting that the working-class O'Casey was a socialist as well as a republican. None of the tenement-dwellers of O'Casey's plays gains anything from the fine speeches and sacrificial acts of the true believers, whether in Ireland or war zones abroad.

In one of the most provocative scenes in his Easter Rising play *The Plough and the Stars*, the pub conversation of prostitute Rosie Redmond is intercut with the offstage speechifying of the rebel Patrick Pearse, who is rallying the troops outside the pub: "The old heart of the earth needed to be warmed with the red wine of the battlefields," Pearse declaims, "And we must be ready to pour out the same red wine in the same glorious sacrifice, for without shedding of blood there is no redemption" (98). Rosie may describe this as "th' sacred thruth, mind you, what that man's afther sayin," but she is more pressingly concerned by the loss of her trade now that the men's minds are on politics rather than pleasure (97). The deflationary use of spliced dialogue here recalls the celebrated scene in *Madame Bovary* in which the high-flown language of lovemaking of the caddish Rodolphe is brought forcibly down to earth at the local agricultural show when it is suddenly interrupted by the announcement of the prizewinning pigs at the agricultural fair. Pearse becomes the political equivalent of the finely spoken but fundamentally dangerous and dishonest Rodolphe.

The emphasis thus far on poetry and drama should not be taken to imply that there was no significant modernist fiction about the years of conflict in Ireland. On the contrary, Nicholas Allen has taken novelists as canonical as James Joyce and Samuel Beckett to show why it is significant that the establishing of the Irish Free State coincided with the modernist *annus mirabilis* of 1922, arguing that what both Irish modernism and the Free State shared was their rendering problematic in new ways the relations between the subject and the community. For Allen, this problem is at the heart of Irish modernism, when in post-Independence Ireland "failure was inscribed in the avant-garde. Beckett, Joyce and Yeats tuned into the possibility that the difficulty of writing was writing difficulty, their readers and their society forced to rethink themselves in [the] face of an unrecognisable art" (16–17).

There were more direct representations than this of the crisis. With a reputation as a war writer at least since Heather Bryant Jordan's *How Will the Heart Endure* (1992), and consolidated by her inclusion in major studies of Second World War writing by Gill Plain and Phyllis Lassner, the Anglo-Irish Elizabeth Bowen is also among the novelists who have benefited from the recent chronological expansion of the modernist canon (as a "late modernist"). In *The Last September* (1929), Bowen presented a penetrating treatment of divided political loyalties during the crisis in Ireland. This atmospheric novel follows the coming of age of a marriageable young Anglo-Irish woman, Lois Farquar, during the end stages of the British occupation. In his novel *A Drama in Muslin* (1886), Irish transitional or proto-modernist George Moore had set his semi-satirical treatment of the Irish marriage market against the violent backdrop of the 1880s' land reform movement, which everyone is struggling to pretend is not happening. A thunderstorm breaks overhead at a Dublin ball, for example, and "[e]veryone thought instinctively of dynamite" (176); and the assassination by land reformers of his ennobled brother turns the otherwise unappealing Mr. Burke into the Marquis of Kilcarney and the prime target for the novels' socially ambitious mothers. In Bowen's novel, too, public violence both intersects with and offers a pointed critique of the limited familial aspirations of Ireland's decaying gentry. But as the characters in Bowen's doomed country estate of Danielstown await the demise of their whole way of life, the coming of the rebels starts to carry an almost erotic charge: "some lovely certain excitement, as of the first approach to the War," thinks one character (121); another, lying in bed, "longed for the raiders" (152).

Lady Naylor's ostensibly throwaway comment about how "all young people ought to be rebels"—a heavily freighted term in this context, to say the least—is more serious than it seems (173). Throughout the novel the loyalties of the Anglo-Irish characters are surprisingly hard to pin down. For a start, the older characters with the most to lose in the independence struggle identify surprisingly unselfconsciously as Irish, as when one refers to "our national grievances" against the English (178). They experience long-standing if feudal (and probably sentimentalized) intimacies with their tenants; thus, for the sake of his dying mother, they are dismayed when the occupying English soldiery capture the rebel Peter Connor. And then there is their class-inflected contempt for the English soldiers upon whose protection they depend. Thus Lady Naylor rules out the Surrey subaltern Gerald Lesworth as a suitor for Lois, explaining that she finds English people "very difficult to trace" genealogically—by which she means socially (80). Bowen wrote in another context of the "snobbishness" of her Anglo-Irish class, who "did not always admire the England that they did not fail to support" ("The Idea of France" 63). This characteristic set of negations on Bowen's part captures well the attitude of the Anglo-Irish in *The Last September*.

And so, interestingly, the novel's main casualty is the English soldier Gerald, with his futile love for Lois and his ignoble occupation of protecting British and Anglo-Irish interests. A conversation with Lois's lazy, cynical cousin Laurence, an Oxford undergraduate who prides himself on his modern intellectual credentials, reveals Gerald's simple, conservative, and irretrievably passé imperial patriotism:

> "Well, my opinion is—
> "Oh, but I don't want your opinion, I want your point of view."
> "Well, the situation's rotten. But right *is* right."
> "Why?"
> "Well ... from the right point of view of civilisation. Also you see they don't fight clean."
> "Oh, there's no public school spirit in Ireland. But do tell me—what do you mean by the point of view of civilisation?"
> "Oh—ours."
> Laurence smiled his appreciation: the conviction, stated without arrogance, had a ring of integrity. Gerald, embarrassed by this benevolence, had recourse again to the back of his head, so gratifyingly polished. "If you do come to think," he explained, "I mean, looking back on history—not that I'm intellectual—we *do* seem the only people."
> "Difficulty being to make them see it?" (132–3)

Innocent Gerald mistakes for approval Laurence's condescendingly amused "appreciation"; he lacks the modern irony about which Laurence is so vain, and adheres instead to a wholly unsophisticated belief in the manifest superiority of Englishness and empire that he assumes Laurence must share.

Gerald's physical beauty compounds the slightly kitsch effect of a patriotic Rupert Brooke who has outlived his time: he is "pleasant ... and rather pretty. He is like a photograph of a man in an advertisement" (75). Women fantasize about his death; at a tennis party two spinsters "hoped he would not be shot on the way home; though they couldn't help thinking how, if he should be, they would both feel so interesting afterwards" (49); a little later, Lois "thought of death and glanced at his body, quick, lovely, present and yet destructible" (128). "Nothing could make him into a tragedy," Lois says of Gerald, and if events prove her wrong in one sense—he is murdered—the narrative nonetheless proves her correct at the same time because Gerald is killed somehow unheroically and, above all, not in the least tragically (91). The section of the novel in which he dies in a rebel ambush is titled merely "The Departure of Gerald," whereas in the same chapter, and in marked contrast to the "departure" that is Gerald's, the house of Danielstown is burned to the ground in a rebel arson attack described, in terms more appropriate to the human damage of the war, as an "execution" by "executioners" (303).

Gerald's death feels as though it ought to mean more than it does. What finally marks the difference between modernist war writing and modernist writing about political violence outside of the structures of war is really this question of how far death can rhetorically be transformed into something truly meaningful. When, in "The Burial of the Dead," the speaker of *The Waste Land* memorably asks his former comrade Stetson if the corpse buried in his garden has "begun to sprout? / Will it bloom this year?" Eliot stands for many modernist writers in reinstating the materiality of the putrefying corpse as a way of refusing war's logic of overwriting last year's dead bodies with this year's political abstractions (55). The transfiguration of sacrifice is a much more conflicted affair in writing about non-sanctioned violence: we are forced to ask not only how far it is acceptable to aestheticize the dead, but also what to do with the dead when they have already aestheticized themselves. Of all modernist works, it is Yeats's most famous poem on the Easter Rising that addresses this most explicitly when it examines a stylized rebellion that turned political action into an artistic statement by transfiguring its participants from ordinary people into heroes and martyrs. "A terrible beauty is born," Yeats so famously wrote in September 1916 of the dead insurgents:

> I write it out in a verse—
> MacDonagh and MacBride
> And Connolly and Pearse
> Now and in time to be,
> Wherever green is worn,
> Are changed, changed utterly:
> A terrible beauty is born. (205)

Somewhere between a half-disbelieving record on recent events ("I write it out in a verse") and a performative decree about what these events are coming to mean ("Now and in time to be"), the poem participates in a national mythologizing ("Wherever green is worn") of an event whose brutality and apparent futility it nonetheless finds impossible to approve.

4

Journeys to a war

*"Who will you be sending to Ishmaelia?" asked Mrs Stitch.
"I am in consultation with my editors on the subject. We
think it a very promising little war. A microcosm as you
might say of world drama."*
EVELYN WAUGH, *Scoop* (14)

*And maps can really point to places
Where life is evil now.
Nanking. Dachau*
W. H. AUDEN and CHRISTOPHER ISHERWOOD, *Journey to a War* (253)

It was more than appropriate that Paul Fussell followed up his classic *The Great War and Modern Memory* with a study of interwar travel-writing, *Abroad* (1980), given the extent to which war and travel came to intersect in the later part of the period associated with modernism. Fussell opens *Abroad* with eloquent passages from English trench writers, unwillingly "abroad" already, fantasizing about the warmth, light, and color of Mediterranean travel, and ends with the transformation of the interwar travel book into the war book at the end of the 1930s. Travelling increasingly became a form of witnessing, and travel writing a kind of war reportage in the 1930s. As the decade went on, many important English-language writers left home not to escape their own shores but to watch the approach to their shores of the crisis that would end the decade: they went to Spain and Germany, but also to Abyssinia and Yugoslavia, and wherever they went became, as in that mocking line from Waugh—, novelist, travel-writer, and former war correspondent—a "microcosm ... of world drama."

"How old-fashioned you are with your frontiers," a failed Communist revolutionary announces in Graham Greene's first novel *Stamboul Train* (1932): "The aeroplane doesn't know a frontier; even your financiers don't recognize frontiers" (149). The writing of war and violence in the 1930s suggests a threatening collapse of borders whereby foreign crises feel no longer capable of containment as something happening elsewhere, and to other people. When we look at writers' attitudes toward the wider world what we find is a tendency for the almost natural and unspoken cosmopolitanism of modernism to shade into a more nervous geopolitical consciousness, and a more urgent sense of the ties between one's own nation and others. This chapter shows that 1930s modernism is as much concerned with war and violence as was the literature produced around the Great War. What focusing on the war-travel book will make clear, though, is an important change of style as writers experiment with documentary and hybrid modes, and a change of perspective as the imperial center-and-periphery model that survived through the European Civil War of 1914–18 gives way to apprehensions of genuinely global transformation as the force of new ideological formations such as Communism and Fascism begins to emerge.

New perspectives on modernism and the "interwar"

Points of continuity and discontinuity between the war-haunted modernism of the 1920s and the simultaneously postwar and prewar literature of the 1930s have attracted substantial critical attention in recent years. Kristin Bluemel has coined the term "intermodernist" for the generation of writers who followed high modernism and who, although often influenced by modernist precursors, took what she argues is a more overtly political and activist turn. In her volume on this topic, she defines intermodernism in accordance with three elements—cultural, political, and literary: intermodernists are more interested than their precursors in the working-class and the working aspects of middle-class life; they are often politically radical; they are more inclined than modernists to borrow from popular forms of writing (1). Topics that her volume covers indicate the significance of state power, of the international outlook, and of war and violence for thinking about the "intermodernist": essays on Storm Jameson and the idea of Europe; interwar travel; wartime spy fiction; Elizabeth Bowen and war crimes; Rebecca West and witnessing, and so on. Instructively, Bluemel uses as her own opening "intermodern" case study a war book, Richard Hillary's memoir, *The Last Enemy* (1942).

Bluemel uses the term "intermodernism" in an avowedly promotional way; it is a way of using the institutional capital of modernism to draw attention to mid-century writers who have typically received less attention than their precursors. Nonetheless, it is also a serious effort to work through the relationships between literature and political engagement in the interwar period. Increasingly, though, it is hard to sustain the traditional dichotomy of an aesthetically minded 1920s and a politically committed 1930s—a dichotomy created by, and most useful to, the 1930s writers who were trying to get out from under the shadow of their formidable predecessors. Not only is it hard to sustain in the face of decades of work on modernists' real-world engagements, but also in the face of much more nuanced versions of the 1930s than the 1930s writers—who were their own best publicists—offered. Much work on the interwar revises the relationships between the generation who defined the 1930s and the older writers identified so canonically with the 1920s, and the influence between generations is more emphasized now; it is even a two-way influence for if, to take Steve Ellis's example in *The English Eliot* (1991), Eliot influenced the early Auden, then Auden influenced the later Eliot. Of all the common ground those writers shared, the experience of living through extraordinarily violent times must be counted as especially influential, in the years when the traumatic aftermath of one world war shaded into apprehensions of the next.

How the interwar environment shaped the late modernism of the 1930s and 1940s is the subject of Thomas Davis's recent *The Extinct Scene* (2015), which argues that modernist techniques were repurposed to register world-systemic distress in literary representations of ordinary life in Britain "in a historical period plagued by extraordinary crises" (3): "the Sino-Japanese war, the expansionist policies of fascist states and a civil war in Spain that destabilized the continental equilibrium Britain so needed, and transformations in sovereignty and political belonging wrought by decolonization and mass migration after the Second World War" (16). Responses to disorder manifest themselves for Davis in a range of hybrid new forms: modernist surrealism feeds into Britain's 1930s efforts at domestic anthropology such as the Mass Observation project and the film documentary movement, for example, while 1930s novels such as Woolf's *The Years* and Isherwood's *Goodbye to Berlin* combine the weak plots of modernism with the expansiveness of the historical novel, the travel book becomes the fragmentary and inconclusive war travel book (*Journey to a War, Homage to Catalonia*), and modernist antirealism takes a gothic turn as it registers the insecurity of civilian life in the Second World War (Henry Moore, Elizabeth Bowen).

So as distinctions between 1920s and 1930s writing come to seem less important than they once were, distinctions between realism and experiment begin to break down. For example, Davis follows a number of critics in understanding the "realist" documentary movement in the 1930s as continuous with modernism; he describes how the documentary film "put the avant-garde at the service of the liberal state" (34) when Scottish filmmaker John Grierson worked through the 1930s with the Empire Marketing Board and the General Post Office, both government agencies, and when Humphrey Jennings produced in wartime some of Britain's most distinguished propaganda alongside the Ministry of Information—as Davis puts it, "a disarticulation of adversarial politics from avant-garde aesthetics" (66). This was not an uncommon development: we find a similar blend of experiment and accommodation, document and invention, in Virginia Woolf's hybrid *Between the Acts* (1941). The novel is set in 1939 in the grounds of a country house where a pageant of English literary history is being staged and, in contrast to the sense of alienation marking Woolf's earlier treatments of the national culture, this is a novel about an England exasperatedly loved because newly endangered by the planes overhead ("And what's the channel," one character asks, "if they mean to invade us?" [135]).

Numerous critics have discussed the overlap between modernism and documentary in the 1930s. Laura Marcus discusses the film and literature of 1930s "documentary culture" in terms of "its intertwinings of a modernist aesthetic and a realist imperative, a poetics and a politics" (205); Tyrus Miller describes a "tense complementarity of modernist and documentary modes" evidenced particularly strongly in the surrealist or surrealist-inspired interwar prose poem (229); film historian Bill Nichols has argued that an essential but disavowed aspect of the documentary film was its deployment of potentially disruptive modernist elements of juxtaposition, defamiliarization, and fragmentation (580–610). As critics follow the afterlife of 1920s modernism into the troubled and violent mid-century, what once looked like a break with modernism starts to feel more like a reformulation of it.

Benjamin Kohlmann's recent monograph on left-wing literature in the 1930s, *Committed Styles* (2014), also does much to complicate traditional readings of high modernism's relationship to the succeeding decade. Kohlmann's target is two of the most durable clichés about the 1930s: first, that modernism was systematically and unproblematically renounced in the 1930s by the interwar Left as a privileging of bourgeois and individualist formalism, and, second, that only at the end of the decade did writers, disillusioned, renounce the project of an interventionist political literature. On the contrary, Kohlmann argues that even writers whom we think of as among the most doctrinaire of the decade were haunted by ideas of aesthetic autonomy that they themselves had done so much to shore up when they wrote about their predecessors. This near-nostalgia for a literature that is accountable to none but itself is what Kohlmann calls the "apolitical unconscious" of 1930s writing (3).

Of particular relevance for thinking about late modernism and war is Kohlmann's nuanced reconstruction of the interwar career of William Empson, a writer whose poetry had been published in the left-wing periodical *New Signatures* and who yet, unlike the dominant voices of his generation, is most usually associated with forms of political detachment rather than commitment. Kohlmann argues that Empson's post-Cambridge travels—which is to say, his exposure to war—were transformative. A stint teaching in Japan and then from 1937 to 39 in China, as invading Japanese troops approached and sent his university into flight, led him to review his ostensible poetic neutrality. In "Autumn on Nan-Yüeh" (1940), parenthetically subtitled "(with the exiled universities of Peking)," Empson finds that it is not, after all, "shameful to aver / A vague desire to be about / Where the important things occur" (79). Kohlmann finds that Empson was divided between "the urge to escape from the political and military broil and the desire to take his stand on one side of the ideological divide" (89), and this poem is a particularly compelling instance of Empson's ambivalence. Having announced in the ninth stanza his dislike for "The verses about 'Up the Boys,' / The revolutionary romp, / The hearty uproar that deploys / A sit-down literary strike" (76), the twelfth stanza opens with the hesitant "Politics are what verse should / Not fly from" (77), the line break and the negation marking his hesitation to commit—but also his commitment even in the face of that hesitation.

Besides, he asks himself, if he really believes in "this passive style," "what / In God's name are you doing here?" (79). Empson had not left England actively or intentionally in pursuit of a foreign war to witness or record, but was caught up in it involuntarily by force of historical circumstance. Christopher Isherwood's hybrid novel/story collection *Goodbye to Berlin* (1939) is also about a somewhat inadvertent witnessing in that it documents the last days of the liberal Weimar Republic, although writing a book on the rise of Nazism would not have been Isherwood's primary intention when he took up residence in the Berlin demimonde. *Goodbye to Berlin* even jokes about the question of motive when Christopher's English pupil Hippi Bernstein asks him what he is doing there and he is driven to "improvise" unconvincingly that the "political and economic situation ... is more interesting in Germany than in any other European country" (260–1). (Hippi's father, meanwhile, may or may not be deliberately teasing him when, to the visible amusement of his own gay son, he asks Isherwood for his views on the persecution of Oscar Wilde for his homosexuality.) "I am a camera with its shutter open, quite passive, recording, not thinking," Isherwood famously begins, and if what emerges is far more artful than this opening implies, a substantial part of the power of *Goodbye to Berlin* is the way in which it conveys the kind of passivity that comes from the impossibility of knowing how events are going to work themselves out while you are living through them (243). From the perspective of the early 1930s, the Nazis are populist thugs—but are they something even worse than that?

More canonically "thirties" were the travels to China that produced Isherwood and Auden's *Journey to a War* (1939), in that, as the title suggests, this journey represented a wholly active decision to seek out conflicts raging outside the British Isles, often conflicts that were loaded with symbolic significance in the light of a widely expected second world war. China would be "a war all of our very own," Auden told Isherwood, reflecting the relative lack of interest among Anglophone writers in what was happening in the Far East (*Christopher and His Kind* 299). Inevitably, some of these writers' works suggest that genuine political engagement and activism were mixed up with a generational pathology among those who had been too young to fight in the First World War, or "the Test," as Isherwood symptomatically put it in one of those self-accusing confessions so typical of 1930s autobiography:

> Like most of my generation, I was obsessed by a complex of terrors and longings connected with the idea "War." "War," in this purely neurotic sense, meant The Test. The test of your courage, of your maturity, of your sexual prowess: "Are you really a Man?" Subconsciously, I believe, I longed to be subjected to this test. (Parker 100)

Even Orwell, an iconic figure in his resistance to forms of political mystification, seems to be self-consciously trying to relive an older generation's experience when, early in *Homage to Catalonia* (1938), he describes preparing for the battlefields of Spain as if he were readying himself for the wet trenches of northern Europe in 1918. But *Homage to Catalonia* is very much a book about getting things politically wrong, and about writing as an effort to put the record straight, which means that Orwell's own initial misconceptions about the purity of the struggle between the Left and Right in Spain are inevitably part of the story he tells.

Taking sides on Spain

When Auden offered Isherwood "a war all of our very own," the implied contrast would have been with the Spanish Civil War, which had mobilized the political interests of many writers. It would be difficult to overstate the historic importance of this conflict in studies of Anglophone writing in the 1930s. As Valentine Cunningham wrote in his landmark *British Writers of the Thirties* (1988), "If there is one decisive event which focuses the hopes and fears of the literary '30s, a moment that seems to summarize and test the period's myths and dreams, to enact and encapsulate its dominant themes and images, the Spanish Civil War is it" (419). "Today the struggle," Auden announced in his subsequently revised and then uncollected poem "Spain." And for many the contest between the elected socialist government of Spain and the Fascist coup of General Franco looked like a dress rehearsal for the war that would determine the political future of Europe (52). Writers often imagined themselves as bearing the torch for this truth in the face of the indifference of their neutral (British or American) governments. Here, we might think of John Dos Passos's and Ernest Hemingway's collaboration on the script of Joris Ivens's work of propaganda *The Spanish Earth* (1937), although the huge contemporary popularity of *For Whom the Bell Tolls* (1940), published when the outcome of the war was accepted as a Fascist victory, reminds us that their propaganda aims were only one aspect of English-language writers' interest in the Spanish Civil War.

The way in which the Spanish Civil War has been canonized has meant that a narrow group of Anglo-American responses has obscured the Spanish ones (and the canonical English-language writers were not necessarily very interested in these), a point made by a number of recent critics, including Jessica Berman (185) and Gayle Rogers (164). Rogers's study of modernism and Spain has illuminatingly shown how Anglophone responses to the war should be viewed in relation to a longer history of British and Spanish literary and cultural engagements between the wars, when Spain served as a testing ground for ideas about the cultural map of Europe and the fate of cosmopolitanism in a continent ravaged by the Great War. Thus, the Spanish Civil War is one interwar moment among a number of others, albeit the most violent and consequential, where sympathetic British onlookers transform Spain into a symbol of something else. Davis was not exaggerating when he wrote that the "Spanish Civil War ascended to high allegory" (119), and that its political complexities were subsumed even by the most passionately invested of onlookers into a generalized struggle for "the preservation of high ideals like democracy and freedom over fascism and barbarism" (120).

Both Berman and Rogers discuss Woolf in the context of the Spanish Civil War, an important reminder that writers could give sustained thought to the situation in Spain without leaving home, given the extent to which the Spanish Civil War was a modern media war, and communications from Spain made their way into writers' studies. Woolf had known Spain at firsthand only as a tourist, and Rogers explains that, up until the Civil War, hers was substantially an exotic tourist's eye view of the country ("an amalgam of her own impressions and recycled tropes from England's cultural imagination" [129]), but, as he also goes on to note, Woolf and her husband were among the first British intellectuals to protest publicly about the fascist attack on the Second Republic in the summer of 1936 (146).

As sensitive in her own way as Orwell to the relationships among political rhetoric, cliché, and the difficulty and necessity of resisting forms of co-optation, Woolf begins to write extensively around this time about the extent to which the febrile public language of war can colonize the inner life even at a distance. In the "Present Day" section of her novel *The Years* (1937), the aftermath of the Great War and the approach of the next war collapse into one another. Accompanied by her niece Peggy, elderly Eleanor Pargiter passes the statue of "a woman in nurse's uniform holding out her hand":

"The only fine thing that was said in the war," she said aloud, reading the words cut on the pedestal.

"It didn't come to much," said Peggy sharply. (319)

Readers are expected to recognize the nurse as Edith Cavell, executed by the Germans during the Great War, and to know that the words on the pedestal are Cavell's famous declaration that patriotism is not enough. That "it didn't come to much" is evidenced in the fatigued omission of the details, as if they are too wearily familiar to be worth remarking now that, as Peggy later says, "On every placard at every street corner was Death; or worse—tyranny; brutality; torture; the fall of civilization; the end of freedom" (368). Spain has brought violence home again. The problem here is that the threat is real ("tyranny; brutality; torture"), but the language is the same old sloganeering ("the fall of civilization; the end of freedom") that everyone of Peggy's crisis-fatigued generation has heard before.

The companion piece to *The Years*, Woolf's famous pacifist essay *Three Guineas*, is her work most explicitly engaged with the Spanish Civil War, but its aim is to reflect on what this war means in the context of others—in the hands of Anglophone writers in the 1930s, symbolization was the usual fate of foreign wars. Published in 1938, the time of its writing is reflected in its concern with propaganda and the mobilizing manipulation of emotion in wartime. In his 1937 essay "Spilling the Spanish Beans," Orwell wrote that this conflict had "probably produced a richer crop of lies than any event since the Great War of 1914–18," but with the essential difference from the First World War that the progressive left-wing press had proved itself as capable of intellectual dishonesty as such counterparts on the Right as those who had rejoiced in Hun-bashing atrocity stories in the Great War (269). This sense that no side is wholly to be trusted runs throughout Woolf's *Three Guineas*, and it finds famous political expression in Woolf's proposal for an "Outsiders Society" of those who can best serve the causes of peace and justice by refusing to take sides at all, by observing "an attitude of complete indifference" to war—which is, naturally, easier said than done (122–3).

In *Three Guineas*, crucially, it is not simply that words have been co-opted by partisans on all sides—the Great War had given her generation a shattering education in the distortions of political discourse—but also the visual image. Here again emerge the distinctive problems posed by 1930s documentary, with its hard-to-evaluate combination of subjectivity of perspective and authenticity of presentation. Woolf writes early in her essay of those pictures of war atrocity that the Republican government in Spain "sends ... with patient pertinacity about twice a week":

> They are not pleasant photographs to look upon. They are photographs of dead bodies for the most part. This morning's collection contains the photograph of what might be a man's body, or a woman's; it is so mutilated that it might, on the other hand, be the body of a pig. But those certainly are dead children, and that undoubtedly is the section of a house. A bomb has torn open the side; there is still a birdcage hanging in what was presumably the sitting-room, but the rest of the house looks like nothing so much as a bunch of spillikins suspended in mid air. (13–14)

Attesting to the foundational significance of the Spanish Civil War for modern photojournalism, Susan Sontag used this passage from Woolf to open her well-known essay on the visual representation of war, *Regarding the Pain of Others* (2003). Sontag emphasizes two main aspects of the passage. First, she questions Woolf's contention that war photographs are "simply a crude statement of fact addressed to the eye"; to the participants, Sontag points out, the obliterated human subjects of war photography are not universalized "innocent victims of war" but victims with a political identity—in our time, for example, Israeli or Palestinian (10). Second, Sontag presses on the "we" of Woolf's address who respond to images of war with shared revulsion:

> Who are the "we" at whom such shock-pictures are aimed? That "we" would include not just the sympathizers of a smallish nation or a stateless people fighting for its life, but—a far larger constituency—those only nominally concerned about some nasty war taking place in another country. The photographs are a way of making "real" (or "more real") matters that the privileged and the merely safe might prefer to ignore. (7)

Here, Sontag ironically invokes Neville Chamberlain's notorious "faraway people of whom we know nothing" to describe the extent to which "knowing nothing" of "some nasty war taking place in another country" has become decreasingly possible. "Being a spectator of calamities taking place in another country is a quintessential modern experience," Sontag writes (18), and Spain was "the first war to be witnessed ('covered') in the modern sense: by a corps of professional photographers at the lines of military engagement and in the towns under bombardment, whose work was immediately seen in newspapers and magazines in Spain and abroad" (21).

Others have homed in on this visual dimension. Berman has written that *Three Guineas* differs from Woolf's prior work in its "apparent documentary impulse," even as it also confounds with substitution its own tendency to documentation (63)—for example, we never see the photographs of atrocities in Spain to which Woolf refers, although the text includes photographic evidence of English patriarchal power, such a member of the judiciary, and a university procession. One reason why the documentary is an object of suspicion, it is implied, is because of the degree to which it is complicit in the emotional and political aims of propaganda. The visual image purports to possess a neutral status it cannot legitimately claim: after all, if photographs were not arguments for British intervention in support of the Republic why would the Spanish Government send them out with "patient pertinacity" every few days?

Although Woolf was extremely attentive to what was happening in Mussolini's Italy and Hitler's Germany, both of which countries she knew and whose political degeneration she followed closely through the newspapers, *Three Guineas* reverses the 1930s habit of travelling to a war because the book is primarily concerned with outlining how the international situation might be seen as an expanded version of power relations at home. Unlike her ultra-mobile male counterparts, she is looking at the seeming periphery of Spain to see not what Europe could become, but what it already is. For reasons Rogers makes clear, the struggle in Spain against Franco's reactionary forces would have had particular resonance for the feminist Woolf, given that the Second Republic had done so much to (literally) enfranchise Spanish women. Conservative power relations such as those that Spanish women are forced again to confront are to be found at home, in every sense, in that Woolf finds in the private and domestic sphere in England what her left-wing male contemporaries have associated with fascist dictatorship abroad.

She argues in *Three Guineas* that "the public and the private worlds are inseparably connected; that the tyrannies and servilities of the one are the tyrannies and servilities of the other" (162), quoting a newspaper correspondent urging employers to take on male employees and send the women workers back to the home:

> Dictator as we call him when he is Italian or German, who believes that he has the right whether given by God, Nature, sex or race is immaterial, to dictate to other people how they shall live ... Are they not both the voices of Dictators, whether they speak English or German, and are we not all agreed that the dictator when we meet him abroad is a very dangerous as well as a very ugly animal? And he is here among us, raising his ugly head, spitting his poison, small still, curled up like a caterpillar on a leaf, but in the heart of England? (61–2)

Seen from one angle, we could take Woolf's miniaturizing of international crisis as a message with the usual despairing implications of the liberal's conventional "dirty hands" argument—if the same forces prevail at home as abroad, then who are we to contest foreign tyrannies? Seen from another, we could take her perspective as a higher form of political intervention for the very same reason: that to eradicate the spitting, toxic "caterpillar ... in the heart of England" is a step toward improving the world at large.

The writer's platform and its critics

But what we do not find in Woolf is a readiness to take the platform and replicate what she thought of as the hectoring strain of the writers more usually associated with the 1930s, the writers who used to be summed up as, thanks to the title of Samuel Hynes's influential 1976 book, "the Auden Generation." And so her name is missing from the iconic British literary-political document of the decade that emerged when, in the summer of 1937, a group of signatories including Auden, Nancy Cunard, and Stephen Spender wrote "to the Writers and Poets of England, Scotland, Ireland and Wales" to ask if they were "for, or against, the legal Government and the People of Republican Spain? Are you for, or against, Franco and Fascism? For it is impossible any longer to take no side" (*Authors Take Sides* n.p.). The very terms of the question marked it as an implied criticism of modernist elders—albeit, as I have already suggested, an apolitical modernism of this 1930s' generation's own symptomatic making:

> It is clear to many of us throughout the whole world that now, as certainly never before, we are determined or compelled to take sides. The equivocal attitude, the Ivory Tower, the paradoxical, the ironic detachment, will no longer do. (*Authors Take Sides* n.p.)

"Ivory Tower" was a classic way of diminishing immediate predecessors. In the course of its history, the term had slipped from meaning poetic isolation to referring to the secluded quads of Oxbridge before making a comeback in the 1930s to refer to artistic rather than academic forms of self-isolation above the political fray. The 1930s writers made it a cliché: Woolf plays with it in the title of her deeply ambivalent essay on the writers of the decade, "The Leaning Tower" (1940), and when Evelyn Waugh travesties Cyril Connolly's modernist-sympathizing journal *Horizon* in a wartime novel—more of both in the next chapter—the title he gives it is *Ivory Tower*.

Waugh later described the 1930s as a time when "[c]ertain young men ganged up and captured the decade" ("Two Unquiet Lives" 394), and an important part of the reconsideration of the decade has been the reinstatement of its major women writers, many of whom shared the deeply held political convictions of their canonized male contemporaries. With regard to the relation between war and travel, of particular interest is the socialist and internationalist Storm Jameson, whose novel *Europe to Let* (1940) voiced her solidarity with Czechoslovakia, a small but exemplary post-1918 democracy betrayed by its British and French allies in the Munich non-settlement. The following year saw the publication of Rebecca West's encyclopedic *Black Lamb and Grey Falcon*, a condensed (although still 1200 pages in length) and lightly fictionalized account of her travels in another post-1918 European state, Yugoslavia, and dedicated "To my friends in Yugoslavia who are now all dead or enslaved" (n.p.). A committed nationalist *and* a passionate internationalist, a declared socialist who feared and disliked the Soviet Union even in the era of apologism on the Left, the highly complex West can complicate in turn our sense of the Left/Right binaries of the interwar period. Bernard Schweitzer discusses West at length in *Radicals on the Road* (2001), a study of travel writing of the 1930s that offers many useful reminders that conflict-minded travel in this period was undertaken by writers of a whole range of political, and politically volatile, orientations.

After all, it is worth reminding ourselves that there were itinerant 1930s writers who were not on the Left. Like many of those contemporaries, the conservative satirist Waugh had also travelled to a war, reporting on the 1935 Italian invasion of Abyssinia, a country he already knew from covering the coronation of Haile Selassie in 1930. These trips found their way into his largely pro-Fascist and multiply redrafted travel book *Waugh in Abyssinia* (1936), and, much more readably, into his farcical novels *Black Mischief* (1932) and *Scoop* (1938). In *Black Mischief*, a recurring Waugh villain, the opportunistic Basil Seal, decides to go to the beleaguered African kingdom of Azania where the modernizing Emperor Seth, BA Oxon, is trying to avoid a civil war. "Every year or so there's *one* place on the globe worth going to where things are happening," Basil Seal explains: "The secret is to find out where and be on the spot in time" (112). This is the logic of Auden and Isherwood's "a war all of our very own," and catches effectively its opportunistic note.

Nonetheless, in Waugh's satirical version of political events, knowing absolutely nothing about a place and its people is no barrier to writing about them. Early in *Black Mischief*, news comes through to London that Seth has assumed the crown of Azania and journalists churn out copy in accordance with the established commonplaces:

> In Fleet Street, in the offices of the daily papers; "Randall, there might be a story in the Azanian cable. The new bloke was at Oxford. See what there is to it."
> Mr Randall typed: *His Majesty B.A ... ex-undergrad among the cannibals ... scholar emperor's desperate bid for throne ... barbaric splendour ... conquering hordes ... ivory ... elephants ... east meets west* ... (87)

In *Scoop* all the other war correspondents reporting on crisis in a fictional East African state know that the celebrity war correspondent to beat is Wenlock Jakes, the American awarded the Nobel Peace Prize for what seem to be largely fictitious accounts of foreign wars. "Jakes" is archaic US slang for lavatories, and Waugh's character is no better than a feted fraud:

> "Why, once Jakes went out to cover a revolution in one of the Balkan capitals. He overslept in his carriage, woke up at the wrong station, didn't know any different, got out, went straight to a hotel, and cabled off a thousand-word story about barricades in the streets, flaming churches, machine guns answering the rattle of his typewriter as he wrote, a dead child, like a broken doll, spreadeagled in the deserted roadway below his window—you know." (92–3)

That "you know" is telling: war reportage has its clichés, and these strongly recall the Spanish Civil War. Fabricating a version of what they know foreign wars are expected to look like is enough to satisfy a readership back home about the horror of the scene and, naturally, to confirm the attendant courage of the correspondent.

Political travel, then, itself becomes a period cliché. Waugh's friend Anthony Powell, a novelist who had made his reputation in the 1930s, subjects the whole idea of journeying to war to mockery in his retrospective *A Dance to the Music of Time* (1951–75). In the fourth novel of the series, *At Lady Molly's* (1960), set in the 1930s, the narrator's aristocratic friend and future brother-in-law discovers and embraces radical politics while quietly refusing to give up all but the most superficial symbols of his privilege. Known officially as Lord Warminster, to his family as Erridge, to his political allies as Alf, and to the popular press as the Red Earl, this character goes to China for a close-up view of the Second Sino-Japanese War. Erridge then—inevitably—heads off to Spain. In a development typical of Powell's series, his aristocratic family reacts with hilarity rather than horror: "I can't think that Erry would be any great help to any army he joined, can you?" his sister asks, since Erridge is a notorious hypochondriac (*At Lady Molly's* 63). Their reaction is continuous with their attitude to all his previous scrapes: they are delighted when he runs off to China with the common-law wife of a Communist journalist protégé because this is the first time he has shown any interest in women; they take boastful pride in his classically 1930s "down and out" slumming, and rather than downplay the potential embarrassment of what Erridge calls his "social research" (29) when he travels around England examining economic conditions in the 1930s they find it hilarious to tell everyone that their eccentric brother is "[l]iving as a tramp" (27). Orwell's *Down and Out in Paris and London* and *Homage to Catalonia* are clearly Powell's models here for Erridge's quixotic political enterprises, but it is worth noting that Powell was so close a friend of Orwell that he had arranged the funeral after Orwell's untimely death a decade earlier. The partisan political lines were never quite as sharply drawn in the 1930s as they appeared to be.

In any case, a war was something Britain's writers no longer had to travel to find as the 1930s drew to a close. The flight away from war was more attractive, and Robert Hewison describes the emigration of Auden and Isherwood to the United States in January 1939, when the Second World War looked like a foregone conclusion, as "the most important literary event since Spain" (8). In view of the relationship between war and travel in the 1930s, it also seems symbolically apt that one of the first British novels of the Second World War (and, as Jeremy Treglown further points out, "not only in a chronological sense" [111]) should be about the difficulty of taking what was once an easy journey to Britain's closest continental neighbor. The rich, spoiled, bored characters of Henry Green's novel *Party Going* are trying to get to France but are trapped by fog in the London railway terminus. Civilian travel across land and sea seems now to have been supplanted by travel through the air, or, in the spatial perspective the novel habitually mimics, the course of a bomber across the sky. The novel opens with a bird falling dead from the sky and the narrator routinely adopts the bomber's-eye view on events: "Fog was down to ground level outside London, no cars could penetrate there so that if you had been seven thousand feet up and could have seen through you would have been amused at blocked main roads in solid lines, and on the pavements within two miles of this station, crawling worms on either side" (388). Green's deliberately unpleasant use of "amused," accompanied by the dehumanizing image of urban pedestrians as "crawling worms" makes it clear that this aerial view offers, at best, an amoral perspective on the lives of the nameless citizens below. Late in the novel a character reflects on the sinister possibilities of hundreds of people trapped in the same metropolitan space: "What targets," he announces, "what targets for a bomb" (483).

So strongly does *Party Going* apprehend the threat presented by aerial bombing that even as its plot builds up to what has begun to feel disproportionately like a close-run survival—in that the fog lifts and the characters finally get to leave the station—its imagery casts the disaster as already having happened. "My darling, my darling," one character rushes up to another, "in this awful place I wondered if we weren't all dead really" (414). Looking down from above—this narrator looks from above with ominous frequency—at the refugee-like characters perched on their suitcases, the narrator tells us that they are "like ruins in the wet, places that is where life has been ... tumbled down with no immediate life and with what used to be in them lost rather than hidden now the roof has fallen in" (497). Images of a bombing about to happen are shot through with imagery of a bombing that seems already to have happened. An auxiliary fireman who believed that he was likely to die amid London's burning rubble, Green intuited about the coming decade what his contemporary Stephen Spender would soon declare outright: "the background to this war, corresponding to the Western Front in the last war, is the bombed city" (Mellor 2). As the coming chapter indicates, the modernism of the Second World War confirms Spender's insight.

5

Modernism and the Second World War

You say that I am repeating
Something I have said before. I shall say it again.
Shall I say it again?
T. S. ELIOT, *East Coker* (187)

The repetition was senseless, hideous, stupefying.
VIRGINIA WOOLF, *Between the Acts* (67)

Only in recent years have the writings of the 1940s become a relatively mainstream topic in modernist studies. Even the Second World War, the literature of which ought to have been readily compatible with enduring modernist interests in problems of violence and representation, attracted the tenacious cliché Paul Fussell quotes that it was "a war to which literature conscientiously objected" (*Wartime* 133). For a surprisingly long time this was passed over as a period of silence or, at best, underachievement, when compared to the literary profusion of the previous war. "War can't produce poetry, only poets can ... War can only in subject matter affect poetry," Dylan Thomas defensively announced, responding presumably to the pressure to live up to First World War writing—although, ironically, some of his own best-known poems were written during the Second World War (561). "Where are the war poets?" was the literary hack's question of the early 1940s, and the standard answer now is the same as that Cyril

Connolly gave in his *Horizon* editorial on the topic in 1941: "under your nose" (5). After years of new attention to the formerly neglected mid-century period, sometimes but not exclusively from critics associated with modernist studies, the view that the Second World War produced no major writing to compare with its predecessor is now impossible to sustain. What is more, a war that has often been identified as an endpoint for modernism is now understood by many as, if not wholly assimilable to modernism, then at least continuous with the experiments of the previous twenty years.

Many writers of the Second World War held the comparison with predecessors at the forefront of their minds. Adam Piette writes in *Imagination at War* (1995), his important early recuperation of the period, that the literature of the Second World War was "too often dismissed as a dry rerun of the First, without anyone bothering to query what this might mean" (2). What, then, does it mean? Clearly the pressure of comparison exerts itself with special force on soldier poets, given their inheritance from the writers of the Great War. Some were acutely conscious of this lineage. The gifted Keith Douglas, a veteran of the North African war who was killed at Normandy while still only in his early twenties, is a symptomatic example of the Second World War writer's hyperconsciousness of what earlier war poetry had been able to do and say. Douglas not only acknowledged his debts to these forerunners within the poetry itself (in his poem "Desert Flowers," flowers blooming amid death prompt him to concede "Rosenberg I only repeat what you were saying" [108]), but also announced in "Poets in this War" that everything had been said before:

> [H]ell cannot be let loose twice: it was let loose in the Great War and it is the same old hell now. The hardships, pain and boredom; the behaviour of the living and appearance of the dead, were so accurately described by the poets of the Great War that every day on the battlefields of the western desert—and no doubt on the Russian battlefields as well—their poems are illustrated. Almost all that a modern poet on active service is inspired to write, would be tautological. (119)

Yet the same essay mocks contemporaries in the safety of wartime Oxford for having "no experiences worth writing of" (119). Indeed, Douglas was so much, if somewhat perversely, influenced by trench forerunners that his war memoir *Alamein to Zem Zem* implied that it was precisely *because* he was a poet that he sought out active service, escaping from his relatively safe job behind the lines to join his regiment in battle. "I never lost the certainty that the experience of battle was something I must have," he wrote: "Whatever changes in the nature of warfare, the battlefield is the simple, central stage of the war: it is there that the interesting things happen" (5). On the staff side there is nothing "to excite a poet" (6). This was a countereffect of their writing that the trench poets of the prior war might not have anticipated: "All a poet can do today is warn," Owen had famously written, but a new generation perhaps took the brutal and sublime form of their warnings as a perverse inspiration ("Preface" 98). Herbert Read, a veteran of the Great War, had expressed his concerns about exactly this phenomenon: "The more effectively war is reported as literature, the more attractive war itself becomes" (xiv).

We can see, then, why the comparison with the Great War is relevant for thinking about the war writers of 1939–45, given how important it was for how they thought about themselves. What about noncombatant writers? In what ways, and to what effect, does their writing in the 1940s respond to the "secondness" of the Second World War? I suggest in this chapter that modernism itself was also self-consciously resurrected in the Second World War. In a sense, this should not be particularly surprising given how many major modernists of the 1910s and 1920s were still producing major poetry and prose, although for institutional reasons—some quite simple, to do with how and what we teach, and why—their later work lacks the straightforward canonicity of their 1920s writing. However, there is another way in which critics have seen the literature of the Second World War as a literature of recurrence, because so much of it explicitly recalls the traumas of the First World War and its aftermath. High modernist images of broken minds in broken cities take on a retroactively prophetic quality in the 1940s when the long-anticipated bombers arrive.

Thoughts on modernism in 1940

Reflections on the meanings of the First World War were commonplace in the literature of the late 1930s. By now it had become obvious that a new war was virtually inevitable, even in the face of antiwar efforts ranging from popular pacifist movements such as the Peace Pledge Union to the broad acceptance of the government's policy of appeasement. Outside of the literary, this late 1930s interest in the relationship between the First World War and the prospect of another showdown with Germany found expression in a whole range of media in these closing years of the tenuous peace. In *The Truth about the Peace Treaties*, serialized in the Conservative-leaning *Daily Telegraph* early in 1938, former prime minister David Lloyd George tried to defend himself from what had already become a historical truism that the coming war was a result of Versailles's supposedly Carthaginian peace. Outside of Britain, the same year saw the remake of Abel Gance's harrowing *J'Accuse*, a 1919 film about war guilt and what is owed to the dead. What the original version had left as an open question is now answered: the sacrifices of the earlier war were indeed in vain. In George Orwell's *Coming Up For Air* (1939), a veteran of the First World War is appalled to see a younger generation throw itself into war as unthinkingly as his own generation had: "Of course he's spoiling for a war," George Bowling thinks of a young anti-fascist speaker: "How can you blame him? For a moment I had a peculiar feeling that he was my son, which in point of years he might have been. And I thought of that sweltering hot day in August when the newsboy stuck up the poster ENGLAND DECLARES WAR ON GERMANY, and we all ... cheered" (179). Orwell was no appeaser, nor was he a pacifist, as his service in Spain had shown, but in this novel he denounces through his mouthpiece George Bowling the truth that the First World War had done nothing in the long run to mitigate the bellicose instincts of ideologues.

By now, Orwell, in his own voice, was among a number of writers working to historicize the literature of the century's first half in relation to its engagements with war and violence—and of course I began this book with a very different one, Wyndham Lewis, who published *Blasting and Bombardiering* in the late 1930s. The war's first year saw two major essays from writers of different generations, styles, and interests on the ways in which the experience of war had shaped modern literature: Orwell's "Inside the Whale" and Virginia Woolf's "The Leaning Tower." Both writing in 1940, Woolf and Orwell independently set out to explain the difference between the modernisms of the 1920s and the political writing of the 1930s, and both essays underscore the significance of the Great War. Woolf argues that the fundamental difference between her 1920s contemporaries and the writers associated with the 1930s is between a generation that had known stability—her own—and a generation that had not. The year 1914 was an extraordinary trauma, Woolf acknowledges, but it arrived too late to be truly formative for the writers who would dominate the 1920s: "when the crash came in 1914 all those young men, who were to be the representative writers of their time, had their past, their education, safe behind them, safe within them. They had known security; they had the memory of a peaceful boyhood, the knowledge of a settled civilization" ("The Leaning Tower" 113). In contrast, those whom she terms the "leaning tower" writers, still children in the Great War, had never experienced peace, and arrived at intellectual maturity knowing only ominous political turbulence all around:

> When they looked at human life what did they see? Everywhere change; everywhere revolution. In Germany, in Russia, in Italy, in Spain, all the old hedges were being rooted up; all the old towers were being thrown to the ground. There was communism in one country; in another fascism. The whole of civilisation, of society, was changing. There was, it is true, neither war nor revolution in England itself. All those writers had time to write many books before 1939. But even in England towers that were built of gold and stucco were no longer steady towers. The books were written under the influence of change, under the threat of war. ("The Leaning Tower" 114)

Writing of these 1930s successors, Woolf walks a rather fine line between disparagement and compassion: "Who can wonder if they have been incapable of giving us great poems, great plays, great novels? They had nothing settled to look at; nothing peaceful to remember; nothing certain to come"; their times have made them anxious and self-aware by driving them "into self-consciousness, into class-consciousness, into the consciousness of things changing, of things falling, of death perhaps about to come" ("The Leaning Tower" 120).

Orwell's late essay "Why I Write" confirms Woolf's thesis, in that he claimed there that the historical times through which he lived had "forced [him] into becoming a sort of pamphleteer" despite that he would have loved to have written ornate and decorative works such as, implicitly, those of Woolf's generation (313). (This may be wishful thinking, of course, since his least well-thought-of novels are the ones most indebted to modernist narrative forms.) In "Inside the Whale," he had already reached a verdict on the interwar period that was compatible with Woolf's. In Orwell's terms, the "tragic sense of life" that dominated the modernism of the postwar 1920s gave way to ideas of "serious purpose" as the keynote for the following generation. As Orwell presents them in "Inside the Whale," the 1920s modernists looked with unrivalled intelligence into everything they could conceivably interpret in psychological and philosophical terms, but turned their eyes altogether from the political present:

> There is no attention to the urgent problems of the moment, above all no politics in the narrower sense. Our eyes are directed to Rome, to Byzantium, to Montparnasse, to Mexico, to the Etruscans, to the Subconscious, to the solar plexus—to everywhere except the places where things are actually happening. When one looks back at the 'twenties, nothing is queerer than the way in which every important event in Europe escaped the notice of the English intelligentsia. The Russian Revolution, for instance, all but vanishes from the English consciousness between the death of Lenin and the Ukraine famine—about ten years. Throughout those years Russia means Tolstoy, Dostoievsky, and exiled counts driving taxi-cabs. Italy means picture-galleries, ruins, churches, and museums—but not Blackshirts. Germany means films, nudism, and psycho-analysis—but not Hitler, of whom hardly anyone had heard till 1931. In "cultured" circles art-for-art's-saking extended practically to a worship of the meaningless. (228–9)

After decades in which critics have been unpacking the political commitments and real-world social interests of modernist writers, it is obvious how selective a picture Orwell is offering of the 1920s: to render modernism apolitical was a strategically useful caricaturing for writers of Orwell's generation as they tried to remove themselves from the shadow cast by their extraordinary predecessors. What is more surprising, though, is how Orwell makes this sketch of an inward-looking and historically unseeing modernism serve a more interesting objective than simply doing down the modernists. On the contrary, it allows him to license the retreat in 1940 from the political rallying of the 1930s writer. Through a laudatory reading of the belated American modernist Henry Miller—introspective, obscene, bohemian, expatriate—Orwell's essay defends the new relevance of a kind of writing that might have seemed extinct in 1940. In fact, Orwell argues that the apolitical inwardness and subjectivity of Miller's fiction are a perfectly appropriate response to the 1940s insofar as they endorse the importance of the individualistic and the idiosyncratic at a time when these are becoming harder than ever to protect as legitimate ends in themselves. Miller's renascent modernist tactics offer resistance to the forms of political collectivization and homogenization that the liberal Orwell feared would only tighten their hold on culture in wartime—and especially afterward, hence his famous announcement in "Inside the Whale" that in the new era of totalitarianism the novel is "as surely doomed as the hippopotamus" (250). And by "the novel," what Orwell has in mind is not "pamphleteering," as he called it, but the novel of wayward interiority and free subjectivity that he associated with modernism.

Patrick Deer writes in *Culture in Camouflage* (2009), his wide-ranging study of late modernism and the state war machine, about the intellectual resistance writers mounted to being co-opted for the work of normalizing the nation's war. Orwell's 1940 defense of the private and independent concerns of Miller against the party-line imperatives of political commitments or the national interest place Orwell in the more obviously aestheticist company of Cyril Connolly, who is an important figure for thinking about the renewed relevance of modernism in the 1940s—less as a creative writer (which he also was) than as an influential critic and editor. Connolly was a member of the same generation as Orwell but, although leftish by declaration, his interest in the political aspects of the aesthetic had never been much more than half-hearted. Modernism—or, rather, the values the 1930s generation attached to modernism—would return in the shape of Connolly's new literary and cultural magazine, *Horizon*, whose first issue appeared in January 1940: "Our standards are aesthetic, and our politics are in abeyance," he announced in his inaugural editorial (5). Readers offered their own verdict on what this meant, Connolly dryly reported in the following issue, where he described how *Horizon* had been accused of modernist aestheticism, or "going back to the twenties" (68). He may have been recalling ironically Cecil Day Lewis's "Letter to a Young Revolutionary" (1933): "These nineteen-twentyish germs must be expelled from my system. Who are they to tell me that I must not preach?" (28). In the end, these germs had never been expelled from the system of mid-century British culture, and British culture may have been all the better for them, given the demands for consensus that war makes. As a response to war, *Horizon* could certainly be described as a kind of modernist recidivism, but for the Anglophile Paul Fussell in *Wartime*, his study of American and British culture in the Second World War, it spoke to what remained robustly independent in a period when so much pressure was on Allied cultural producers to mobilize in the service of the state: "The whole operation, which published some of the finest writing during the early years when Britain was widely assumed to be losing the war, constitutes one of the high moments in the long history of British eccentricity. As a cultural act, it was as stubborn as Churchill's political behavior" (211).

The cultural importance of *Horizon* in its time is evidenced in its appearances in fiction about the period, hence, for example, its appearance in Ian McEwan's retrospective war novel, *Atonement* (2001), where McEwan has a fictional Cyril Connolly reject the writer-protagonist's early and, ironically, too derivatively modernist efforts. True to form, Evelyn Waugh offered the most astringent view of the *Horizon* enterprise in his retrospective war trilogy, *Sword of Honour* (1952–61), where *Horizon* becomes *Survival* and Cyril Connolly, Everard Spruce:

> The war had raised Spruce, who in the years preceding it had not been the most esteemed of his coterie of youngish, socialist writers, to unrivalled eminence. Those of his friends who had not fled to Ireland or to America had joined the Fire Brigade. Spruce by contrast had stood out for himself and in that disorderly period ... had announced the birth of a magazine devoted "to the Survival of Values." The Ministry of Information gave it protection, exempted its staff from other duties, granted it a generous allowance of paper, and exported it in bulk to whatever countries were still open to British shipping. Copies were even

scattered from aeroplanes in regions under German domination and patiently construed by partisans with the aid of dictionaries. A member who complained in the House of Commons that as far as its contents were intelligible to him, they were pessimistic in tone and unconcerned in subject with the war effort, was told at some length by the Minister that free expression in the arts was an essential of democracy. (513)

Waugh was writing this well after the war, and his snapshot of the political utility of the little magazine as a symbol of "free expression in the arts [as] an essential of democracy" feels a little anachronistic, as though the Second World War were being reinterpreted through the perspective of the cultural Cold War. This is particularly apparent when we are told later in the same novel that "since Hitler had proclaimed a taste for 'figurative' painting, defence of the cosmopolitan *avant garde* had become a patriotic duty in England" (596). Here, the postwar reader swaps Hitler for Stalin, figurative for socialist realist, and reads this version of *Horizon* backward through (what we now know of) the funding of *Encounter* under the editorship of Stephen Spender. But long before that, in *Put Out More Flags* (1942), the same lack of overt political engagement gets the editor of the apolitical *Ivory Tower*, another cruelly funny satire on *Horizon*, forced into flight when his now old-fashioned modernist neutrality gets mistaken for fascist sympathies because he rewrites its formerly anti-Nazi conclusion when a mischief-maker tells him that it resembles "the sort of stuff American journalists turn out by the ream" (245). There, the aesthete Ambrose Silk is hopelessly out of his time in attempting to uphold artistic values irrespective of the implied political tendencies of the work he writes and publishes.

Second-wave modernism

Notwithstanding Waugh's mockery, Connolly was more in step with his time than even he could have known when he founded *Horizon*: in the Second World War, modernism was unexpectedly back. Many of the finest literary productions of the war were the works of modernists writing late in their careers: in terms of the novel, we might think of, most canonically, Virginia Woolf's *Between the Acts* (1941), published a few months after her death, and in poetry T. S. Eliot's *Four Quartets* (1943), one of the major publishing events of the war, and imagist H. D.'s (Hilda Doolittle's) long Blitz poem *The Walls Do Not Fall* (1944), with its conflations of architectural, bodily, and emotional ruin. Thinking about a quasi-canon of Second World War modernism, we would also want to include those works produced in terrifying wartime circumstances on the Continent, such as Samuel Beckett's *Watt* (1953), the substance of which was written when the Resistance member Beckett was on the run in the south of France. Most famously, among the older modernists, Ezra Pound's *Pisan Cantos* (1948) were written, as Pound puts it in the poems, "from the death cells in sight of Mt. Taishan @ Pisa," the product of his incarceration for treason at the hands of US forces at the end of the war (5).

There is a sharply recursive and revisionist dimension to these late modernist works, and Pound (who had good reason to believe that he was going to be executed) looks back here on, for example, his old friendships with other modernist writers. Seen from one angle, *The Pisan Cantos* are not nearly revisionist enough, given that they are defiantly pro-fascist even in the face of fascism's defeat; seen from another, they have a subjective and autobiographical quality that much of Pound's other work does not. As Michael Alexander implies, what makes the *Pisan Cantos* more readable than they might be is that Pound's "active political judgement" is so comprehensively discredited there that one no longer needs to pay much attention to it (Pound's "crankiness stands revealed for what it is"); that what stands out is the poetry's "unprecedented emotional freedom and force" as political theorizing and Olympian myth-making give way to Pound's newly autobiographical efforts to think through his own frightening and humiliating circumstances (193).

John Whittier-Ferguson's *Mortality and Form in Late Modernist Literature* (2014) offers an elegant treatment of Second World War modernism as the work of writers whose reputations had been made decades earlier. Focusing on the late works of Woolf, Eliot, Lewis, and Gertrude Stein (who spent the war in Vichy France, a story told in Barbara Will's *Unlikely Collaboration* [2011]), Whittier-Ferguson describes how these ageing modernists reassessed their previous work to take their writing in new directions, offering new ideas about literary form.

> Turns and returns marks these texts in quite different ways—at the level of syntax, in stylistic details and thematic elements, and in larger poetic and narrative forms. The writers' memories of their own writing lives and of the Great War that they lived and wrote through in their late twenties and early thirties conspire to mark these later works with repetitions. "Make it new"—already, of course, an ancient command, brought out of the archive and dusted off when Ezra Pound first recovered and broadcast it—might be more aptly formulated, for the period with which this book is concerned, as "Make it again." And even that phrase, less hortatory than its earlier version, can easily become for each of these authors also a question resonant sometimes with determination, sometimes with despair: "Make it again?" (6)

This is another way of approaching the secondness of the Second World War, and Whittier-Ferguson's book goes on to describe the formal corollaries of a self-conscious lateness as "literary modernism coming to terms with itself, its inheritances, and its legacies" (8). His opening example is a strikingly original reading of Woolf's final novels, books in which not so much as "a sentence … could be mistaken for something Woolf would have written in the 1920s" (10); ironically, this is because she is interested in cultivating not the original but the already used: "the world's ordinary language … passing platitudes, hackneyed phrases, received ideas, and familiar, if botched, quotations from English literature" (9). The repetition of world war finds expression in a preoccupation with repetition at the level of narrative texture, for "revisions and repetitions may be about all that's left" (15).

In addition to those already very established writers, thinking about late modernism and the Second World War we would need to take into account those we might think of as the "second-generation" modernists who produced some of their most important work during the war, such as the poet Wallace Stevens and novelists such as Elizabeth Bowen. A thoroughly original writer who came into his own only in the Second World War, Henry Green is an important figure in this move toward the extension (and not just recapitulation) of modernism.

In the late 1930s and still in his own early thirties, Henry Green was writing his self-lacerating experimental memoir, *Pack My Bag*. Published by the Woolfs' Hogarth Press in 1940, this is perhaps the subtlest and most engaging literary treatment of how the childhood experience of the First World War shaped a generation's expectations about the coming Second World War. Woolf, in the same year, described this generation as one that had never known peace, and from its very first lines *Pack My Bag* asserts the definitive impact of previous wars on the self-understanding of those writers who experienced the Great War as children:

> I was born a mouthbreather with a silver spoon in 1905, three years after one war and nine before another, too late for both. But not too late for the war which seems to be coming down upon us now and that is a reason to put down what comes to mind before one is killed, and surely it would be asking much to pretend one had a chance to live. (1)

Pack My Bag is an evasive text on its most expected material: autobiography. It deliberately avoids proper names, for instance, even when they are easily discovered. But like its perhaps unconscious model, Robert Graves's war memoir *Good-Bye to All That* (1929), it is unsparing on remembered embarrassment—and, increasingly, on what it means to feel that you have let other people down. (Can it be true, as Green declares, that "the story of Judas ... haunts all little boys"? [81].) Green emphasizes the public uses of shame in his account of his wartime school days: "If we did wrong we were reminded they were out there fighting for us" (35); "a habit which lasted well into what we called the Peace, of reminding boys every Sunday of the fathers, brothers and uncles who had died for them" (79). But it is when, during his school holidays late in the war, he returns to his aristocratic family's home that war guilt becomes truly personal, for now, in 1917, the medieval Forthampton Manor has become a convalescent hospital for shell-shocked soldiers where his family "were feeding them up to go back to be killed" (60). Some of these men were "nearly dead ... people meant to die" (61). With cold horror Green remembers a shell-shocked soldier who was "no longer human when he came to us"; he suffers a fall when Green takes him out for a bike ride, and the twelve-year-old

Green blames himself: "it did not do him any harm but it damaged me" (63).

> Unattractive in every way, small, ugly, with no interests one could find, he had haunted eyes as though death to which he was still close and which walked arm in arm with him through our meadows could be a horror worse than what he was still suffering. He did not sleep, he hardly ate, he shook all day and he was like an old specimen jar which is cracked and irreplaceable, others are made which may be better but they do not know how to make them the same, so cracked that a shout will set up vibrations enough to shatter it in jagged pieces, so that if one laughed he always screamed. If forty yards away you banged the door he screamed. (62)

Green's was clearly a generation shaped by war, but *Pack My Bag* goes further than recounting the effects of war experienced and anticipated, in that it reflects on the extent to which the imminence of the Second World War may have altered even his most vivid memories of its precursor: "This feeling my generation had in the war, of death all around us, may well be exaggerated in my recollection by the feeling I have now I shall be killed in the next" (74).

By the time he published *Pack My Bag*, Green was an auxiliary fireman in London, and had reason to imagine not surviving the war: in conditions of wartime blackout the fires set by one bomb immediately become outstandingly visible targets for the bombers who follow them, jeopardizing the lives of the men fighting the first blaze. But notwithstanding the seeming certainties about his doom in *Pack My Bag*, when Green wrote about his actual experience as an auxiliary fireman in his remarkable late modernist novel *Caught* (1943), what he insisted upon were *failures* of anticipation; the volunteer fireman Richard Roe expects to die in the bombing of London, and although he survives physically intact (albeit psychologically damaged) the novel is dominated by projections like those of *Pack My Bag*, projections that shade into a kind of self-dramatization that Green now quietly derides.

In this representative early passage from *Caught*, Roe walks in the rain in the grounds of his country house with his five-year-old son, Christopher. Having now convinced himself that he is going to die in a blitz that has not happened yet, he identifies morbidly with what may be a sick deer (perhaps a "roe" deer) on the estate:

> Then, as they turned to come back, going out of their way to climb along a fallen tree, another herd of deer moved off into the veil, heads up, one of them coughing. He [Christopher] wanted to know if it was going to die. Asking this he struck so close to the note this sad day played over and over, with the wet, the silence once broken, flying low over tops of trees, by a warplane which he did not even look up to watch, neither did the deer, and to the note repeated which was this separation that war had forced into their lives, all these sounded the closing phrase of a call to depart, and Roe said the deer would die, that it was sure to. (6–7)

Caught up, so to speak, in his own tragic sense of himself, Roe forgets that he is talking to a small child; there is no reason to assume that the deer that coughs into the silence is actually dying and not just coughing, and, even if there were, most parents would try to manage rather than indulge a small child's thinking about death. But Roe is only one among many characters in the novel who cope with their unprecedented circumstances through self-dramatization. As they narrate their experience to themselves and others they ensure that they are seen in more romantic or simply more generically recognizable lights. As Michael North describes, each of Green's characters "becomes a simplified version of himself, purposely distorted and reformed to fit the odd, dimensionless context of the war" (*Henry Green* 105).

What North goes on to describe as "the disconcerting tendency toward instant fictionalization of overwhelming experiences" is remarkably prevalent in late modernist fiction (117). Novels such as Elizabeth Bowen's *The Heat of the Day* (1949) and Graham Greene's equally wayward pseudo-espionage novel *The Ministry of Fear* (1943) are full of reflections from characters on the novel-like, as they see it, conditions of wartime London. Stella Rodney in *The Heat of the Day* thinks her own flat looks "like something— possibly a story" (47); dinner with her traitorous lover Robert is likened to "a rendezvous inside the pages of a book" (97); the spy Robert Harrison is "[b]y the rules of fiction ... 'impossible'" (140);

the whole treason plot itself no less than "crazy, brainspun, out of a thriller" (190). Louie Lewis, the other main character in *The Heat of the Day*, spends the war "look[ing] about her in vain for someone to imitate" (15), and is happiest when she recognizes herself in the prefabricated demographics of the wartime newspapers: "Was she not a worker, a soldier's lonely wife, a war orphan, a pedestrian, a Londoner, a home- and animal-lover, a thinking democrat, a movie-goer, a woman of Britain, a letter writer, a fuel-saver, and a housewife?" (152). As Piette has argued, the private imagination proves vulnerable in wartime, perpetually at risk of saturation by the public sphere; the war "hollowed and emptied out the private mind," he writes, "transforming it into a scene of lies, artificial dreams and fabricated emotions" (4). In a number of late-modernist novels about the war, this is clearly operating as a form of psychological insulation.

In Green's *Caught*, Roe's lower-class double, Albert Pye, a regular in the London Fire Brigade, is another self-dramatizer who finds it reassuring to have a socially sanctioned caricature to live up to. Out of his social depth when confronted with a mixed fire station of working-class regulars and middle-class temporary auxiliaries like Roe, Pye casts himself as a salt-of-the-earth hero, as if he would like to be a stereotypical working-class minor character in a more familiar kind of fiction. In fact, what happens in the novel is that this complex and troubled man is psychically destroyed by vivid memories of adolescent incest that may or may not have happened; the obscurity of wartime blackout recalls to him a youthful encounter on a dark night, an encounter so hazily recalled that he convinces himself retrospectively that his sexual partner was his actual sister. Even Mary Howells, the cook at the fire station, rewrites her experience of tackling her errant son-in-law in his barracks about his neglect of her daughter—in reality, they have a cup of tea and the confrontation she initially anticipates and subsequently fabricates never happens—in order to present herself as the fiercely protective working-class mother she knows that she would be in a less complicated and more socially patronizing novel. "The extraordinary thing," Roe concedes at the end of the novel, "is that one's imagination is so literary" (175). The novel was published in 1943, but it is set largely during the Phoney War of 1939–40, and this purgatorial, suspense-laden setting is crucial for thinking about the characters' preoccupations with the roles they will play when the war begins in earnest: they all know that something terrible is about to happen but cannot know what they will become when they are finally tested. Knowledge inherited from the previous war is redundant: Great War veteran Pye's lectures habitually recur to the last war as if he is unconsciously searching for precedents, yet he complains about those "who think this war, if there is one, will be like the last" (16). In this respect, he is obviously correct.

At the end of the novel, the bombing finally starts, and Roe tries to describe to his uncomprehending sister-in-law the conflagration that has led to his invaliding out from the fire service for traumatic stress or "nervous debility" (173). "(It had not been like that at all)," the narrator interrupts in a parenthesis:

> (What he had seen was a broken, torn-up dark mosaic aglow with rose where square after square of timber had been burned down to embers, while beyond the distant yellow flames toyed joyfully with the next black stacks which softly merged into the pink of that night.) (181)

Insofar as it is "like" anything, from the description the narrator offers the reader, it recalls a much earlier scene, when Roe's young son Christopher, kidnapped by Pye's emotionally disturbed sister, finds himself in an unfamiliar sitting room with a blazing open fire in the grate. Again, events are placed in parenthesis:

> (The lady took Christopher into a room. It was very hot. It had a coal fire. He was surprised that she did not take off his things. She crouched by the fire. Looking back over her shoulder, she poked it, saying "the darling, the darling." She did not turn on the light, so that he could see her eyes only by their glitter, a sparkle by the fire, which, as it was disturbed to flame, sent her shadow reeling, gyrating round sprawling rosy walls.) (12)

On some level Roe knows that the two scenes are connected because when he tries to describe his experience of the Blitz he asks his sister-in-law to consider the way in which memory gets overwritten and he turns, as if out of nowhere, to Christopher's kidnapping for an analogy: "When you heard, what did you imagine the room was like that Christopher was in, I mean before the police brought him back?" (175). It is as if the Blitz allows him to access some other prior trauma associated with childhood, for both Christopher's and his father's experiences of fire end with traumas that have been ineffectively confronted. There is a warning for Roe in his son's response to his kidnapping, which is quickly "forgotten, seemingly, done with": that "seemingly" is more a wish than an actuality.

Something similar happens in Green's friend and fellow fireman William Sansom's contemporary "Fireman Flower," the long title story that ends his Hogarth-published 1944 collection. Sansom's fireman protagonist enters a burning warehouse during the Blitz and seems to move back in time to childhood as he does so.

> My task is succinctly—to discover the kernel of the fire. I must disregard the fire's offshoots, I must pass over the fire's deceptive encroachments, and I must proceed most determinedly in search of the fire's kernel. Only in that way can I access efficiently the whole nature of the fire ... (126)

Thus Flower talks to himself on his approach to "the secret he must unravel," but "the seat of the fire" becomes something far stranger when, in anticipation of C. S. Lewis's celebrated fantasy centered on the wartime evacuation of children, *The Lion, the Witch and the Wardrobe* (1950), Flower hacks through the back of a wardrobe and finds himself in a comfortable domestic scene—a fireside in the homely sense—untouched by the fire that consumes the surrounding warehouse. Through this portal, his childhood friend Stephen Chalmers sits by the hearth, surrounded by artifacts from Flower's distant past: his mother's sewing bag, his father's tobacco bowl, the schoolboy Flower's old French grammars. Flower attributes his nostalgic longing to the fact that the past is "secure, closed off ... nothing like the unstable present, which one could hardly understand at all" (149), but perhaps the resort to childhood here and in *Caught* speaks to a lack of control that simply will not fit into adult, rationalizing frames of reference.

Sebastian Knowles titled his study of Second World War writing *A Purgatorial Flame*, following Eliot's "Little Gidding" in describing how the war was felt as somehow cleansing: famously or notoriously, Eliot there transfigures the Luftwaffe bomber into "the dark dove with the flickering tongue" (203). As the examples of Green and Sansom also suggest, a powerful association opens up between fire and psychological revelation in the writing of this period, although perhaps most explicitly of all in Louis MacNeice's Blitz poem "Brother Fire" in which the flames that are destroying London are "enemy and image of ourselves" (196). But, as Piette shows, the poem is not quite the exposé it seems; or, rather, what it is exposing is less an innate truth about the human will to destroy but the utility of both theological rationalizations (the war as purification by fire) and Marxist-materialist explanations (MacNeice's jargon of the "dialectician") for the fire as the instrument of cultural renewal (40).

Piette's survey of the war's poetry and fiction is indebted to psychoanalysis—he introduces it as "a study of the war in the mind" (1)—but he is also highly sensitive to the extent to which psychoanalysis itself was a key resource for the period's writers precisely because this was modernism "after" modernism. Analogies between public and private destructive impulses, homologies between the burning city and the witnessing consciousness, all "slip off the page as easy as butter off a frying pan," Piette notes (46). This is perhaps why psychoanalysis has been as useful and influential for thinking about civilian writing of the Second World War as it has been for discussing the modernisms of the 1920s, with its population of shell-shocked veterans. "A bad war, this," a character says in Greene's *The Ministry of Fear*: "Civilians with shell-shock" (109). Nonetheless, shell shock is not the whole psychoanalytic story of the mid-century experience of war, and, in her reading of late modernism and the generation of psychoanalysts who followed Freud, Lyndsey Stonebridge has argued for the importance of anxiety at this time as "the affective register of a form of historical anticipation" that would have been experienced by far more people than were actually traumatized by war (4).

More recently, Kristine Miller's sociologically minded *British Literature of the Blitz* (2009) discusses Green in relation to the period's interest in violated masculinity and its relationship to social expectations in wartime: Green's Charley Summers in *Back* (1946) and Arthur Rowe in Greene's *The Ministry of Fear* are explicitly trauma cases. *Hors de combat* by necessity—one is a maimed former prisoner of war, and the other is unfit for conscription after years spent in an asylum for the ostensible mercy killing of his wife—these men have no obvious place in a culture of total war, their very citizenship as British men jeopardized by their inability to "do their bit," as the wartime cliché had it. Miller finds in Green's war fiction a concern with "the pressure of sustaining a masculine identity so heavily reliant on the repression of emotional pain," a reading that renders his war novels markedly continuous with the 1920s fictions of shell shock (112). Damon Marcel DeCoste sees a more profound critique of late modernist historical narrative in *The Ministry of Fear*, a novel set partly in a shell-shock clinic, which he sees as engaging modernist views of a cyclical history—violence enacted, violence forgotten, violence reenacted. DeCoste describes the modernist view of history "as tragic repetition" and "the ceaseless rehearsal of past atrocity" (429). Woolf would have agreed, on the basis of the diary entry she wrote while reading Freud at the very end of 1939: "If we're all instinct, the unconscious, what's all this about civilisation, the whole man, freedom, &c?" (*Moment's Liberty* 464). In an especially despairing passage in *Three Guineas* where she likens the modern dictator to the tyrant Creon in *Antigone* she concludes that "Things repeat themselves it seems. Pictures and voices are same today as they were 2,000 years ago" (162). As Sarah Cole writes of Woolf's late work, "Repetition in some basic way means violence; its presence shocks and sickens" (*At the Violet Hour* 280).

But among all the works focused on the recursive qualities of the Second World War Green's treatment of trauma in *Back* could not be surpassed. Charley Summers is a shell-shocked and severely wounded former prisoner of war newly repatriated from Germany to a home transformed in ways he refuses to recognize. Charley's married lover, Rose, has died years earlier, during the week in which Charley was taken prisoner, but (although the novel opens by her grave) he believes her to be still alive. Throughout *Back*, characters try to account for Charley's condition with recourse to their memories of the First World War, but their efforts fail either to explain or console: "They're coming back nervous cases, like they did out of the last war," a character despairs, "and thought that, in that case, then everything was hopeless" (106). The psychic disturbance extends beyond the former soldiers and prisoners, as when the mother of Charley's dead lover cannot distinguish the returned Charley from her own younger brother, John, killed at seventeen in the previous world war ("She will insist it's the last war," her husband explains [15].) Charley, meanwhile, uses the language of the last war to articulate his predicament, thinking himself "as dead as if he were six feet down, in Flanders, under the old tin helmet" (77). All the characters in *Back* readily repeat the psychoanalytic discourse that was once pioneering: "there's compensations in not remembering, as I dare say you've found" (31). The title of *Back* is apt: what has come back at the end of the Second World War is not only the shattered Charley but also the unfinished business of a war that broke out thirty years earlier.

"That the dead of one war haunt the doomed of the next becomes a provocative image for twentieth-century war poetry," writes Tim Kendall (44). His comment clearly holds true for fiction as well, given the extent to which 1914–18 returns in the writing of 1939–45. A number of major writers of the period make macabrely literal that metaphor of "haunting." For example, Storm Jameson's *The Fort* (1941) is set in the spring of 1940, as France fell to the Germans, in a cellar in Northern France, its characters a mixed group of English, French, and German soldiers, some young men and others veterans of the First World War. Only in the novel's final line when the Englishman Ward addresses a young officer as "Jamie," a friend killed in the last war, do we realize that the characters include ghosts of a war fought on exactly the same ground only a few decades earlier. The haunting takes a civilian turn in Bowen's "The Demon Lover," the title story of her 1945 collection of Second World War stories, when the ghost of a dead soldier from the First World War comes back in the Blitz, twenty-five years after his death in action, to reclaim his promised bride. Kathleen Drover is now a middle-aged wife and mother, and, upon returning to check up on the empty London home from which she has evacuated her family during the Blitz, she finds a mysterious letter from "K," a letter reminding her that she had once promised to wait for him. She recalls their sinister parting all those years earlier, but she has forgotten even the face of her former soldier lover until, it is implied, she meets his eyes as he speeds her from her marital home in the guise of the driver of the taxi she has summoned to escape the threatened assignation.

Bowen's war novel *The Heat of the Day* is superficially more realistic, but no less insistent on the ways in which the First World War returns in the Second. The heroine Stella Rodney loses her lover Robert Kelway in this war and has lost her husband, the ironically named Victor, to the previous one; but her losses are stranger than war casualties in the obvious sense: her wounded first husband left her for his wartime nurse (Stella has covered this fact up; like one of Green's self-fictionalizers in *Caught*, she allows herself to be thought the heartless woman who left him instead); her lover in the Blitz either commits suicide or is murdered when he plunges from the roof of her block of flats (Stella covers this up, too, by letting the inquest record his death as a fall).

The Heat of the Day is often misremembered as a novel set during the Blitz—on the contrary, the Blitz is long since over and the action is taking place during what the narrator calls the "lightless middle" of the war (93). If we are inclined to think of this as a Blitz novel, it is most likely because of its memorable flashback to the disorienting context of civilian death in which Stella and Robert meet. This Blitz section is among the novel's most striking passages, where a disfigured prose offers an even more estranging version of Eliot's ghost-walked city in *The Waste Land* ("I had not thought death had undone so many" [55]).

> Most of all the dead, from mortuaries, from cataracts of rubble, made their anonymous presence—not as today's dead but as yesterday's living—felt through London. Uncounted, they continued to move in shoals through the city day, pervading everything to be seen or heard or felt with their torn-off senses, drawing on this tomorrow they had expected—for death cannot be so sudden as all that. Absent from the routine which had been life, they stamped upon that routine their absence—not knowing who the dead were you could not know which might be the staircase somebody for the first time was not mounting this morning, or at which street corner the newsvendor missed a face, or which trains and buses in the homegoing rush were this evening lighter by at least one passenger.
>
> Those unknown dead reproached those left living not by their own death, which any night be shared, but by their unknownness, which could not be mended now. Who had the right to mourn them, not having cared that they had lived? So, among the crowds still eating, drinking, working, travelling, halting, there began to be an instinctive movement to break down indifference while there was still time. The wall between the living and the living became less solid as the wall between the living and the dead thinned. In that September transparency people became transparent, only to be located by the just darker flicker

of their hearts. Strangers saying "Good night, good luck,", to each other at street corners, as the sky first blanched then faded with evening, each hoped not to die that night, still more not to die unknown. (*Heat of the Day* 91–2)

Translated into a drabber mode of expression, the substance of this passage is quite close to a cliché about London during the Blitz: what British people still (albeit with a half-ironic inflection) call "Blitz spirit" when camaraderie emerges out of some catastrophe or other, or the idea that the collective experience of danger and deprivation under fire led to a classless civilian solidarity such as Britain had never seen before. This is what Angus Calder has called, in a book of this title, "the myth of the Blitz," using "myth" to imply not a fabrication but a popular simplification. There is a more straightforward version of this myth in Bowen's 1940 essay "Britain in Autumn," about the high morale of London under bombing, for which she credits "the factor of liking everyone better: everybody is *somebody*, for the first time ... there are no strangers now" (53–4), touching on that question of human recognition to which she returned in the Blitz flashback in *The Heat of the Day*. Even more effusively, she writes, "[w]e have almost stopped talking about Democracy because, for the first time, we *are* a democracy. We are more, we are almost a commune" (54). And yet however familiar the tropes of Blitz democratization and solidarity, Bowen represents the Blitz in a disconcertingly eerie way, with the dead of the previous evening circulating "in shoals." They convey a spectral aliveness that the negation does not quite cancel ("the staircase somebody for the first time was *not* mounting this morning, or at which street corner the newsvendor *missed* a face, or which trains and buses in the homegoing rush were this evening *lighter* by at least one passenger"). Meanwhile the living people in these paragraphs seem less than fully alive; indeed, like ghosts, they are described as "transparent."

Bombsites as "waste lands"

As the example of Bowen attests, writers' efforts to convey the sheer strangeness of the bombed metropolis owe a marked debt to the modernism of decades earlier, and the case for understanding representations of the war in relation to the imaginative models provided by the 1920s is most powerfully made by Leo Mellor in *Reading the Ruins: Modernism, Bombsites and British Culture* (2011). Through his discussion of London-based civilian writers' experience of the Second World War—the war impending, realized, and in its aftermath—Mellor shows the extent to which the modernism of the previous twenty years found both its peculiar actualization *and* its amplification in the smoldering ruins of the city:

> British writing—and culture in general—of the wartime years was dependent in various ways on the aesthetic and intellectual possibilities offered by modernism. There is also one fundamental reason for the centrality of modernism as an active form; for modernism appeared to have been utterly and hauntingly proleptic. Throughout the 1920s and 1930s British writing was filled with ruins and fragments. They appeared in novels, plays and poems as content: with visions of tottering towers and scraps of paper; and also in the *mise en page* shapes of broken poetics and recovered *objets trouvés* phrase shards. But from the outbreak of the Second World War what had been an aesthetic mode began to resemble a template. (5)

And so in the course of his fascinating survey, Mellor describes how, for example, the long-pictured fear of bombing creates a paranoid inwardness and anxiety in fiction of the late 1930s; how the spectacle of the Blitz generated elusive and oblique texts that foreground fiery obliteration as a challenge to textual representation; and how the surrealisms of the 1930s found a new utility in wartime when "a mode that had seemed outlandish and contrived now became an explanatory tool in unprecedented situations, enabling reportage when more conventional tropes appeared debased or inadequate" (93).

"One of the finest of all the stories to come out of the Second World War," according to Bernard Bergonzi's widely shared view (*Wartime and Aftermath* 44), Bowen's Blitz story "Mysterious Kôr" confirms Mellor's thesis about the peculiar aptness of surrealist forms for describing a metropolitan cityscape transformed by violence. In "Mysterious Kôr," London in wartime looks so weird as to be "the moon's capital—shallow, cratered, extinct" (728), because war has re-enchanted the familiar world: "If you can blow whole places out of existence, you can blow whole places into it," as one of Bowen's characters has it (730). In his *British Writing of the Second World War* (2000), Mark Rawlinson presents a more hostile reading of the marked ruin-consciousness of the war's writing, acutely identifying its habit of displacing the more creaturely and less picturesque flesh-and-blood casualties of bombing in favor of architecture transfigured by destruction. Rawlinson argues that "the urban fabric is foregrounded at the expense of human figures," a modernistic move that he views as complicit with the violent forces it might be seen otherwise to critique in that it represents "a striking parallel with the administrative operations of strategic description" (68–9). Whether in the spirit of melancholic elegy or sublime aesthetic, late modernism's emphasis on the damage caused to buildings has, Rawlinson argues, the effect of effacing both the living, made homeless by war, and the dead and damaged bodies created by the bombs that blitzed the buildings.

"I see war (or should I say I feel war?) more as a territory than as a page of history," Bowen wrote in the now-famous preface to *The Demon Lover*, the collection of short stories in which "Mysterious Kôr" appears (5). Bowen, of all the major writers of the Blitz, would have had a powerful sense of the ways in which the spatial transformations created by architectural destruction could be used as metaphor: early in the war, she wrote a memoir of her ancestral Irish home, *Bowen's Court* (1940), and throughout the interwar period she had seen the burning down of such houses by insurgents, as described in her own *The Last September*. As Yeats had it in "Meditations in Time of Civil War," "somewhere / A man is killed, or a house burned, / Yet no clear fact to be discerned" (230). It is not surprising that Bowen should have been so sensitive to habitat, given what good reason the Anglo-Irish had to know how vulnerable to violent destruction an established historic environment could suddenly become. Her war story "The Happy Autumn Fields" oscillates between a late-nineteenth-century Anglo-Irish family and a couple during the Blitz, and, as Thomas Davis writes of this conflation of two different but doomed communities, "Bowen's stories function as expressions of property loss, class levelling, and a coming redistribution of wealth and power," and all these threats are applicable in her mind to both contexts (182).

Some wartime representations of modernism as the new historical reality were more literal-minded than others, and there were works of this period that offered virtually one-to-one correspondences between contemporary experience and the literal language of modernism. Above all others, *The Waste Land*, long since canonical by the 1940s, became the go-to text for writing about life among the ruins. From the title onward, Robert Liddell's novel *Unreal City* (1952) uses Eliot's poem almost as a template for the dislocated, dispossessed, and otherwise shapeless wartime experience of a bereaved English civilian in exile in cosmopolitan Caesarea who is mourning his sister's death in the Blitz. (In one of the novel's oddest allusions to Eliot, one of the main characters in the novel is the sexually disreputable Mr. Eugenides, from Smyrna, naturally, like his forerunner, and he is "the worst person to know—he isn't received anywhere" [18].) Even more insistent on the prophetic qualities of modernism's apocalyptic imagining of violence is Rose Macaulay's *The World My Wilderness* (1949), which is set in 1946 among the ruined churches of central London; the new wilderness of the novel's title is the bombed area around St. Paul's, and it is populated by a range of misfits—deserters, petty criminals, black-market spivs, and other people unable to find a place for themselves in an England trying to put the war behind it. The protagonist, Barbary, and her young half-brother, Raoul, have spent the war with their attractive but negligent mother in France; while their mother has been sleeping with a probable collaborator who is subsequently murdered in regional reprisals, Barbary and Raoul have been running with the local Resistance, and when they are sent after the war to live in London with their eminently respectable father, a judge, and his new wife, they cannot help but introduce into their seemingly safe new lives the trauma and fear with which they have learned to live in Occupied France. *The World My Wilderness* begins with an epigraph from the "What the Thunder Said" section of *The Waste Land*: "In the faint moonlight, the grass is singing / Over the tumbled graves, about the chapel, / There is the empty chapel, only the wind's home," and this opening description of the "chapel perilous" anticipates Barbary's testing herself among London's ruined churches. So from the earliest stages of the novel, and then throughout, the ruins of London are seen through the imaginary ruins that give this section of Eliot's poem its Gothic feeling of a threateningly incomplete abandonment of the city: "these broken habitations, this stony rubbish" (Macaulay 34); "all bats and ghosts ... an' all those windows and doors hanging loose" (Macaulay 120). Indeed, the reader comes to find it somewhat inevitable that *The World My*

Wilderness should end with a character muttering, "we are in rats' alley, where the dead men lost their bones" (177).

What becomes clearest in the course of *The World My Wilderness* is the extent to which the modernist city, and especially the threatening modernist city, gets rediscovered as a privileged means of articulating the traumatic intersection of historical and personal loss. Art historian Stuart Sillars makes a similar point about what he calls "Blitz sublime" in this period's painting when he describes how artists' images of ruin make it possible to externalize the invisible, psychic toll of war (78); for Sillars, the Blitz provided "an external correlative to the familiar state of inner turmoil: external and internal worlds came together to produce a curious and unwonted harmony" (96). We see this confluence of place and trauma at work so comprehensively in *The World My Wilderness* that the war-damaged Barbary proves to be socially and emotionally unfitted for life anywhere outside London's ruins. And when the damaged Barbary finds a kind of spiritual home in the rubble of bombed London, she is coming to recognize the wrecked state of her own mind at the same time as the reader is recognizing a poetic landscape from a century ago: "It had familiarity, as of a place long known; it had the clear, dark logic of a dream; it made a lunatic sense, as the unshattered streets and squares did not; it was the country that one's soul recognised and knew" (40). This paradoxical "lunatic sense" and "clear, dark logic" amount to the antirealism of modernism, as if Macaulay is suggesting that modernism itself was awaiting its fulfillment, or that Eliot's real subject matter was not the war that immediately preceded the publication of *The Waste Land* but a war yet to come.

Given Eliot's status for the younger generation of writers—that is, for the generation that would have to fight the Second World War—perhaps this recourse to *The Waste Land* was almost inevitable. In 1939, the young Sydney Keyes, soon to be killed at the age of twenty in the war in North Africa, would write a poem titled "Meditation of Phlebas the Phoenician," the posthumous thoughts of the "corpse long-drowned," as if Eliot could be repurposed as displaced self-elegy for another doomed generation of gifted young men (104). With his usual satirical acuity, but some hypocrisy, Waugh—himself not averse to borrowing from Eliot, as the title of his interwar *A Handful of Dust* (1934) makes plain—tapped into the prevalent wartime *Waste-Land*-ism in the *Sword of Honour* trilogy. In *Sword of Honour*, his Cyril Connolly figure incorrectly identifies an allusion to Eliot in a poem written by the war-damaged Major Ludovic:

> "There is the Drowned Sailor motif—an echo of the *Waste Land* perhaps? Had you Eliot consciously in mind?"
>
> "Not Eliot," said Ludovic. "I don't think he was called Eliot." (524)

Waugh's morbid joke is that the traumatized Ludovic is not influenced by modernism at all; on the contrary, he is writing realist, testimonial poems about his own near-death and the deaths he witnessed ("I don't think he was called Eliot") on a boat while desperately escaping Crete as it fell to the Germans. Waugh's friend and contemporary Anthony Powell seemed to be recalling this dominance of *The Waste Land* for talking about the Second World War when he, too, wrote a trilogy of war novels, the third "movement" of *A Dance to the Music of Time*. As the wartime trilogy of the twelve-volume series comes to an end, Powell's narrator Nick Jenkins grieves his wartime losses in *The Military Philosophers* (1968) and recalls "the lines about Stetson and the ships at Mylae, how death had undone so many" (113). (But attesting again to the hold *The Waste Land* had on this generation of writers, in an earlier novel of Powell's series, set in the 1920s, Nick has his tarot cards read by a half-sinister, half-comic clairvoyante and expects to draw Madame Sosostris's purely fictional "drowned Phoenician sailor" [*Acceptance World* 11].) To some extent, then, when the modernism of *The Waste Land* was resurrected in the Second World War it was as a poem dissolved into the "fragments" it had disingenuously claimed itself to be within its own lines. It became a set of tropes for talking about the damage of the war, and was put to use with varying degrees of earnestness, from a kind of template-like authority to a joke about the kind of writer who would treat it as a sacred war text. But modernism was also showing itself to be less ossified than this use of Eliot implies. This is where the term "late modernism" is especially useful, and writing about the Second World War offers some of its saddest and most instructive instances.

Tyrus Miller's influential *Late Modernism: Politics, Fiction, and the Arts between the World Wars* (1999) reversed customary teleological perspectives on the history of modernism to look at modernism from the perspective not of its origins—the procedure established by Michael Levenson's groundbreaking *A Genealogy of Modernism* (1984), which was itself an important corrective to modernism's anti-historical self-advertising in relation to the new—but of its radicalized endings against a backdrop of political crisis. Writing as postmodernism itself became history, what Miller found in the often apocalyptic-feeling works of Beckett, Lewis, and Djuna Barnes was an evolutionary link between modernism and postmodernism. This, for Miller, is "late modernism," a term he takes from architectural historian Charles Jencks, who was likewise concerned with the persistence of untimely forms into the middle and later twentieth century.

Where, finally, might the Second World War fit in? We might think, for example, of an experimental war novel such as Günter Grass's *The Tin Drum* (1959), in which comedy and horror are combined in the demonic shrieking and drumming figure of Oskar Matzerath, whose development has been arrested at the age of three, and in which the narratively fantastical and antirealist are intertwined with the tragic and real events in Danzig (Gdańsk) as the Nazis commenced their brutal occupation of Poland. The term "postmodernist" does not really describe the novel—it lacks that end-in-itself, playful, self-referentiality characteristic of, for example, some American fiction in the 1960s—but *A Tin Drum* fits quite well Miller's apocalyptic and darkly comic "late modernism." Or, a second example of an incarcerated child of war, we might think of Nabokov's devastating 1947 story "Signs and Symbols," in which the main character, the child of Jewish refugees from wartime Belarus, would like most of all "to tear a hole in his world and escape" (69). He has been locked up because he suffers from delusions of reference, or the paranoid conviction that everything in his world has a specific meaning in relation to himself. Referential mania, we might say, is a postmodern gesture *avant la lettre*, and for this and other reasons Nabokov might be read as an early postmodernist. But like *The Tin Drum*, this is a war story, first and foremost: these are stories about the children of violence who have inherited in the 1940s a world that has shrunk to the size of their war-broken minds.

Epilogue

Cold War modernism?

In general, something is expected of, or at, the turn of a century. A term of time by being demarcated acquires character, which, as such, makes itself evident as it matures. So a century halfway along its course may be considered due to declare maturity, to have reached culmination-point, to make seen the fruition of its inherent ideas. The twentieth century's development, however, has been in some directions so violently forced, in others so notably arrested as to seem hardly to be a development at all, or at least to be difficult to recognize if it is one.

ELIZABETH BOWEN, "English Fiction at Mid-Century" (321)

HAMM: *And the horizon? Nothing on the horizon?*
CLOV: *(lowering the telescope, turning towards Hamm, exasperated):*
What in God's name could there be on the horizon?

SAMUEL BECKETT, *Endgame* (31)

The deaths of Woolf and Joyce in 1941 have a kind of symbolic significance for how we break up the twentieth century into distinct periods. By the end of the Second World War, almost all the major writers we associate with the first wave of modernism were dead or no longer writing, and many of the experimental writers who followed them would not be canonized until much later, and some not at all. One outcome was that "modernism" would serve for decades as not simply a portmanteau term for a set of aesthetic projects ("Futurism," "Vorticism," "Imagism," and so on) but also as shorthand for the period between 1900 and 1940. Even by the time the Second World War broke out, a consensus had begun to emerge on what modernism "was" and who its drivers had been; thus John Lehmann in *New Writing in Europe* (1940) could reel off the major players of the 1920s and define their achievements without striking a false note: the major novelists were Joyce, Woolf, Lawrence, Stein, and Hemingway, and Eliot was the major poet (15). It was a sincere tribute, but inevitably the sort of tribute that comes close to burying modernism as decisively a thing of the past. The problem of how to describe the period immediately "after" modernism would lie dormant for the next half-century: in the years when modernism was becoming ever more monumental in the critical imagination, the threatening mid-twentieth-century contexts in which its institutionalization took place either went undeclared or were simply forgotten. In closing, I would like to outline briefly some of the ways in which critics have brought these contexts back into view in recent years.

It was probably not by chance that only after the end of the Cold War did it become worthy of remark that modernism's institutionalization in the 1940s and 1950s had coincided with a moment of unprecedented historical anxiety. In *A Singular Modernity* (2002), Fredric Jameson makes the case most stridently that the history of modernism cannot be disentangled from the Cold War: he argues that the ahistorical and emphatically formalist modernism of the old canon, a whole way of thinking about modernism that persisted at least until the 1980s, was the outcome of a fundamentally ideological strategy that used the ostensibly antipolitical for manifestly political ends. Deracinated, dehistoricized, depoliticized, this was modernism as a NATO of the critical imagination, its heterogeneity reified into modern "Western" art. According to Jameson's emphatic formulation, late modernism is "a product of the Cold War" (165). He uses "late modernism" here to refer to two different but intertwined phenomena: first, he is evoking the belatedly experimental work of mid-century and instantly canonical writers like Vladimir Nabokov (whose vehemently expressed aesthetic formalism was conveniently accompanied by the anti-Communism of a dissident Russian-born writer); second, he is describing the retrospective, mid-century reappraisal of the century's first half, which selected those writers most amenable to primarily formalist reading and made them more formalist than they had truly been. It was this Cold War rendering of modernism, Jameson had argued shortly after the end of the Cold War, that had created a "now virtually universal stereotype of the great Western modernists as subjective and antipolitical figures" because "the power of the various aesthetic modernisms was, during the Cold War and in the period of their North American canonization, displaced and invested in essentially antipolitical forms of academic aestheticism" (*Seeds of Time* 118–19).

More than twenty years later, the "virtually universal stereotype" to which Jameson refers is almost unrecognizable, but Jameson was not simply exaggerating for polemical effect. A telling case study here would be Eliot, a writer almost impossible to conceive of as apolitical in the light of his discursive writings: like many midcentury thinkers, he was vitally interested in the notion of "culture" in the democratic postwar West, and his *Notes Toward a Definition of Culture* (1948) is the conservative contribution to a wide-ranging mid-century discussion that historically we often associate with the Left and the emergence of cultural studies. But it is not simply that the work of creating an apolitical formalist modernism entails forgetting the published statements of modernist writers themselves—although it is actually difficult to think of a modernist writer of any significance who avoided the discursive mode so completely that his or her real-life political views cannot reliably be inferred —but that the creative work for which they are canonized was read in such a way as to cut off political readings at the pass. This is the point of John Xiros Cooper's provocative book on Eliot's *Four Quartets*, for example, which describes how critics turned these war poems into a Cold-War-friendly nonrepresentational form, akin to the musical discipline from which they derived their title.

Other critics have dealt more widely with the Cold War uses of modernism. Although the "Cold War" in the subtitle of Robert Genter's *Late Modernism: Art, Culture, and Politics in Cold War America* (2010) is more a period marker than an argument about the emergence of late modernism out of geopolitical crisis, Greg Barnhisel's recent *Cold War Modernists* (2015) returns to the archive to describe the ways in which the meanings of "modernism" changed after the Second World War. As Barnhisel puts it, modernism in the 1950s would "move from being a 'cause' to being a 'style,'" as it came "in support of Western middle-class society" and in service of the cultural Cold War in which East and West battled for cultural influence and "prestige" (2). Barnhisel describes how the disruptive energies and elements that had made modernism appear so shocking and unsettling at the start of the twentieth century got channeled thirty or forty years later into ("Western") notions of freedom, individualism, autonomy, and creative possibility, against the perceived rigidities, collectivisms, and artistic and intellectual servitudes of the Soviet-dominated Eastern Bloc. This happened because modernism was co-opted for the work of cultural diplomacy by official agencies ranging from the United States Information Agency and the Congress for Cultural Freedom to private participants such as the Ford Foundation: "Together, they argued that the very innovation and antitraditionalism that had once made modernist art so threatening to middle-class society proved that Western culture was superior to the new model of culture being forged in the Soviet Union and its satellite nations" (Barnhisel 3). They achieved this by stripping modernism of its political content and modernists of their political affiliations; by divesting modernist origins of their perceived foreignness (lest modernism's cosmopolitan and European sources be construed as "un-American"); and by producing a consumer-friendly modernism of depthless design, play, and ingenuity. But Barnhisel is creditably evenhanded; if what emerged was an intellectually lightweight version of modernism, the whole cultural program of Cold War sponsorship both allowed for the dissemination of modernism beyond the mid-century and brought modernism to audiences it could never otherwise have reached.

When we speak of "late modernism," then, we may be reflecting any number of positions and assumptions: late modernism may be an antipolitical style of writing and a depoliticizing style of reading; it may be a form of state-sponsored distribution. It may simply be a way of capitalizing on the institutional prestige of modernism by expanding its boundaries to incorporate writers whose achievements in their own right have been overshadowed and underappreciated by their belatedness. I, for one, used "late modernism" in this last way in *Modernism and World War II* (2007): if "late modernist" seemed at the time an increasingly uncontroversial and descriptive way to refer to the final major works of Woolf and Eliot, it was also implying approbation for the less familiar authors I discussed.

Of course "late modernist" is not in the least an unproblematic term, and one increasingly important period alternative is "mid-century": a term enjoying renewed critical currency because it appears to describe the period without anchoring it for more or less strategic reasons to other historical moments and critical institutions. "Mid-century" sounds altogether neutral, as if it were merely a means of dating a period. In the context of modernism, war, and violence, however, the term is more loaded than it initially appears to be. As Claire Seiler has pointed out in a stylish reading of Bowen's *The Heat of the Day*, "mid-century" is itself a mid-century invention, which might give us pause because what the term may in fact be describing is not simply a period but the experience of that period from within. Mid-century writers *felt* "mid-century," which is significant, as Seiler shows, because it suggests that the dominant structure of 1940s and 1950s feeling is one of suspension and hiatus.

This is an important insight for thinking about modernism and conflict if we consider why the writers of the twentieth century, unlike those of the centuries before them, should have understood their experience in relation to the least dramatic-sounding temporality of all. On the face of it, suspended middle-ness could hardly be a more negative state: a "nothing" between one "something" and another. Something has *happened* and something is *about to happen*, but nothing is *happening* now. The historical provocation for this sensibility seems almost obvious when we look back at the period in which the Second World War shaded into the Cold War in 1945 and 1946: by the time efforts were being made at Nuremberg to lay the Second World War to rest, relationships between the Allies were already strained by the geopolitical tensions that would dominate the next half century. For those living in the 1940s and 1950s, what has happened is violence; what is about to happen is violence on a potentially world-ending scale. As Robert Jay Lifton wrote in his seminal *Death in Life*, the 1945 atomic bombing of Hiroshima and Nagasaki introduced something new into warfare, and into our thinking about death: "a dimension of totality, a sense of ultimate annihilation—of cities, nations, the world" (14).

"Something is taking its course," says Beckett's Clov in *Endgame* (1957). "We're not beginning to … to … mean something?" Hamm asks in response (32–3). An apocalypse is not a simple ending but a revelation, and of course neither really arrives in Beckett's play. Standing in the background of Tyrus Miller's *Late Modernism* is an apprehension of apocalypse that gives this writing its odd and unassimilable force. We see this in, for example, Miller's haunting descriptions of late modernist works as responses to "high modernism as ruin": they are "disfigured likenesses of modernist masterpieces: the unlovely allegories of a world's end" (14). But perhaps much of modernism was already allegorizing a total ending? Modernism took its course, to borrow Beckett's phrasing, against the background of emergent discourses and actualities of total war.

And definitions of total war have become newly important for thinking about modernism in relation to violence. The emergence of flight has always been within the purview of historicist modernist studies interested in the transformative effects of the period's new technologies: the reality of flight touches on questions of modernity, mobility, and perspective, among many other things. Nonetheless, a more ominous note has crept into criticism in recent years, perhaps because of the ways in which the airplane has been weaponized since 9/11: it was literally weaponized that day, and an ensuing culture of "security" has paradoxically compounded the experience of flight as one of milder or stronger forms of apprehension.

What has become especially clear is that the history of aerial bombing overlaps almost entirely with the history of modernism itself. If the bombing of Guernica and later Hamburg, Dresden, and Tokyo—and then Hiroshima and Nagasaki—has always had an iconic valence, critics have also begun to insist on the fact that aerial bombing had been sanctioned thirty years earlier in a range of imperial contexts, British, French, and Italian. As Paul Saint-Amour incisively points out in his dazzling *Tense Future*, the *annus mirabilis* of 1922 was not simply the year of *Ulysses* and *The Waste Land*, but also the year in which the British started to use aerial bombing ("both threatened and realized") as a form of colonial control in Mesopotamia in order to impose their new mandate in the Middle East (36). Leo Mellor explains that with the development of the "colonial bombsite" as a legacy of what would be euphemized as pacification in Libya, Burma, the Northwest Frontier, Morocco, and Iraq, the "division was to emerge between the 'civilised' and 'uncivilised' areas of the world that would bedevil attempts to limit the role of the bomber—and rationalise the vulnerability of cities—in the years that followed" (12). What both Mellor and more explicitly Saint-Amour are pointing out is that total war is not a fact but a politically consequential rhetorical term: such features of total war as aerial bombing and the erosion of conventional distinctions between combatant and civilian only make a war "total" if they are happening in the metropolis.

By the late 1930s, the aerial threat had comprehensively come home to Europe; here we might think of that hammering recourse in Woolf's *Three Guineas* to the visual record of bombing: "the photographs of dead bodies and ruined houses that the Spanish Government sends almost weekly" (70); "those photographs of dead bodies and ruined houses" (112); "the picture of dead bodies and ruined houses" (161). And it is all coming closer as Woolf writes. Gillian Beer's "The Island and the Aeroplane," an already classic essay on *Between the Acts*, describes how the prospect of bombing eroded the distinctiveness of Britain as an island nation. We see it in the edginess of *Between the Acts*: "The doom of sudden death hanging over us" (114). In keeping with Seiler's point about the self-conscious middleness of mid-century writing, *Between the Acts* is aptly named because it is about a moment in history where life feels horribly suspended, where there is no looking back and no looking forward, or, as one of the characters thinks, using an aptly military formulation, "There is no retreating and advancing" (114). The characters brought together by Miss La Trobe's pageant of English literary history are, we are told, "caught and caged; prisoners; watching a spectacle" (176). What has imprisoned them is precisely the moment in history through which they are living.

And in this period, sky-mindedness becomes almost paralyzing. Picasso's *Guernica* was exhibited in London in October 1938, but by then people did not need reminders of what aerial bombing would look like, nor did they need reminders that the old geographical immunity of an archipelago with a legendary naval fleet would no longer obtain in the age of aerial bombardment. Once, very famously, a way for masses of disparate individuals to come together in the activity of deciphering a script in the sky, Clarissa Dalloway's "strange high singing of some aeroplane overhead" has turned into something else (4). A city in wartime is a threatening thing because groups of people are no longer opportunities for surprising connections among people who seem to have nothing in common but a threat to your own skin; they make you a target for bombers overhead. Here, we might think of the crowds in Green's *Party Going* again ("It's terrifying," says one of Green's sheltered characters: "I didn't know there were so many people in the world" [437]), and recall the overdetermined image of catastrophe from the skies that opens the novel when a pigeon falls plumb dead on the station floor: "One did not seem to expect it when one was cooped up in London and then to fall dead like that at her feet" (394).

The problem with urban crowds in the era of aerial warfare is that masses of people mean masses of bodies. As Peter Stansky has pointed out, the British government anticipated weekly casualties of a completely different order to those that actually occurred: as the war approached, bombs were expected to kill roughly 66,000 British civilians weekly; whereas this was more like the number of British civilians killed in the whole war—an appalling sum in its own right, of course, the disparity between predicted and actual casualties gives some sense of how amplified was the interwar fear of bombing (12). The British government had contemplated the prospect that aerial bombing would kill so many people that the country would not even be able to supply enough wood for the number of coffins required to bury them, a point made with macabre irony in the American Constantine Fitzgibbon's memoir of the Blitz, when he describes contingency planners contemplating "[m]ass burials in lime pits ... even the dumping of bodies from hoppers into the Channel," although given that people were also predicting a complete collapse of civic society under bombardment, "it is hard to see how the corpses could even have been conveyed to the pits" (7).

Mellor has argued for the psychological distinctiveness of what he calls a "prolonged 1939," the period between the Munich Agreement and the outbreak of war (31). His call for the study of this period has since been met in Steve Ellis's *British Writers and the Approach of World War II* (2015), which, in reconstructing the literary and historical contexts of the period between September 1938 and the onset of the Blitz two years later, offers an illuminating account of the interplay between late modernist works and more mainstream phenomena: so, for example, an eve-of-war text such as Woolf's *Between the Acts* (set in 1939) is read alongside the forgotten genre of the post-Munich novel. Ellis takes issue with what he considers the narrowness of Mellor's focus on bomb anxiety as the keynote of 1939 (15), but it is clear nonetheless from his study as well as Mellor's how far the late modernist city is imagined as the site of violent communal death (97–100). In George Orwell's *Coming Up For Air* (1939), London is nothing more than a dense conglomeration of "little red roofs where the bombs are going to drop" (22): "We're just one great big bull's-eye" (24). As Thomas Davis puts it, part of the shock of the 1930s was seeing what happens "when war loses form and the war-making practices Europeans had long reserved for policing the colonies—bombardment, scorched earth, collective punishment—become a normative feature of warfare within Europe" (109).

No longer would there be any notional civilian immunity to war. One terrifying passage from Guilio Douhet's 1921 book *The Command of the Air* is often used to sum up the transformative effect of flight in military contexts:

> By virtue of this new weapon, the repercussions of war are no longer limited by the farthest artillery range of surface guns, but can be directly felt for hundreds and hundreds of miles over all the lands and seas and nations at war. No longer can areas exist in which life can be lived in safety and tranquillity, nor can the battlefield any longer be limited to actual combatants. On the contrary, the battlefield will be limited only by the boundaries of the nations at war, and all of their citizens will become combatants, since all of them will be exposed to the aerial offensives of the enemy. There will be no distinction any longer between soldiers and civilians. (9–10)

These claims seem self-evidently true of modern warfare—that "citizens will become combatants"; that there is to "be no distinction any longer between soldiers and civilians"—but it is untrue as well, and no less painfully so. Enemy civilians may have become as much a target as the soldiers who share their citizenship, but unlike soldiers they themselves cannot kill. Their war is, at most, defensive. Theirs is the experience of pure passivity: the experience of waiting for something terrible to happen, and one of Saint-Amour's most powerful insights is that war inflicts psychic damage long before a single bomb is dropped, through what he calls "weaponizing anticipation" (8). On this reading, air power is structurally analogous to forms of violence ranging from terrorism to torture: the horror is not necessarily what is happening now, but the fearful apprehension of what will. The Cold War kept that apprehension open for another half-century.

And, indeed, modernism perhaps anticipated the threat built into its postwar afterlife, as Jacques Derrida suggested in "No

Apocalypse, Not Now (Full Speed Ahead, Seven Missiles, Seven Missives)," his 1984 paper on the emergent movement toward a "nuclear criticism." A nuclear war would be different not in degree but in kind from previous wars: "Unlike the other wars, which have all been preceded by wars of more or less the same type in human memory (and gunpowder did not mark a radical break in this respect), nuclear war has no precedent. It has never occurred, itself; it is a non-event" (23). Remaining—thus far—in the realms of the imaginary and the textual, a total nuclear war conditions everything and yet has never happened, cannot be compared to anything that *has* happened, and can only be thought about in anticipation for it would leave no witness to record it as an event.

> Thus one cannot be satisfied with saying that, in order to become serious and interesting today, a literature and a literary criticism must refer to the nuclear issue, must even be obsessed by it. This has to be said, and it is true. But I believe also that, at least indirectly, they have always done this. Literature has always belonged to the nuclear epoch, even if it does not talk "seriously" about it. And in truth I believe that the nuclear epoch is dealt with more "seriously" in texts by Mallarmé, or Kafka, or Joyce, for example, than in present-day novels that would offer direct and realistic descriptions of a "real" nuclear catastrophe. (27–8)

For Derrida, modernism gestures toward the "absolute referent": "an absolute nuclear catastrophe that would irreversibly destroy the entire archive and all symbolic capacity" (28); modernism and nuclear criticism is "thought about the limits of experience as a thought of finitude" (30). As Cold War critic Daniel Grausam summarizes this, "for Derrida, fiction cannot ever be mimetically 'about' total nuclear conflict, because no literature that takes seriously the possibility of total destruction could offer speculative postapocalyptic representations of life after nuclear war, which would require survivors to do the representing" (12); all nuclear fiction "*must* be a form of metanarrative that reflects on the very possibility of narrating an event that would leave no narrator" (16). In short, realist forms could never offer a means of representation adequate to the Cold War's new threat of total nuclear annihilation, and the truly nuclear war novel may be the paradoxical product of a preatomic moment.

Modernism, though, was always responding not only to war but reflecting on what it means to write about war. And when it wrote about war, and when it wrote about writing about war, it was always attuned to what *could* happen and not simply what had. In Saint-Amour's words, "violence anticipated is violence already unleashed" (13). I began this book with Conrad's 1905 comments ("Autocracy and War") on the Russo-Japanese War: "More or less consciously Europe is preparing herself for a spectacle of much violence and perhaps of an inspiring nobility of greatness. And there will be nothing of what she expects." Conrad's comments on a local turn-of-the-century war proved more widely applicable in the decades that followed. Wyndham Lewis had promised to explain how it is not only the experience of war that shapes literature, but also a "war about to start." The idea of Cold War modernism points out this moral: that to think about modernism, war, and violence is to consider not simply how literature responds to past events but its orientation toward events to come.

WORKS CITED

Alexander, Michael. *The Poetic Achievement of Ezra Pound*. Berkeley: U of California P, 1979. Print.
Allen, Nicholas. *Modernism, Ireland and Civil War*. Cambridge: Cambridge UP, 2009. Print.
Anderson, Benedict. *Imagined Communities: Reflections on the Origin and Spread of Nationalism*. London: Verso, 1991. Print.
Auden, W. H. "In Memory of W. B. Yeats." *Selected Poems*. Ed. Edward Mendelson. London: Faber, 1979. 80–3. Print.
Auden, W. H. "It Was Easter as I Walked in the Public Gardens." *Selected Poems*. Ed. Edward Mendelson. London: Faber, 1979. 7–8. Print.
Auden, W. H. "Spain." *Selected Poems*. Ed. Edward Mendelson. London: Faber, 1979. 51–5. Print.
Auden, W. H. and Christopher Isherwood, *Journey to a War*. London: Faber, 1973. Print.
Authors Take Sides on the Spanish War. London: Left Review, 1937. Print.
Barnhisel, Greg. *Cold War Modernists: Art, Literature, and American Cultural Diplomacy*. New York: Columbia UP, 2015. Print.
Bazin, Nancy Topping and Jane Hamovit Lauter. "Virginia Woolf's Keen Sensitivity to War: Its Roots and Its Impact on Her Novels." *Virginia Woolf and War*. Ed. Mark Hussey. Syracuse: Syracuse UP, 1991. 14–39. Print.
Beasley, Rebecca and Philip Ross Bullock. *Russia in Britain, 1880–1940: From Melodrama to Modernism*. Oxford: Oxford UP, 2013. Print.
Beckett, Samuel. *Endgame*. New York: Grove, 1958. Print.
Benjamin, Walter. "The Storyteller: Reflections on the Work of Nikolai Leskov." *Illuminations*. Ed. Hannah Arendt. Trans. Harry Zohn. London: Pimlico, 1999. 83–107. Print.
Bergonzi, Bernard. *Wartime and Aftermath: English Literature and Its Background 1939–1960*. Oxford: Oxford UP, 1993. Print.
Bergonzi, Bernard. *Heroes' Twilight: A Study of the Literature of the Great War*. Third Edition. Manchester: Carcanet, 1996. Print.
Berman, Jessica. *Modernist Commitments: Ethics, Politics, and Transnational Modernism*. New York: Columbia UP, 2011. Print.

Bernstein, Michael André. *Foregone Conclusions: Against Apocalyptic History*. Berkeley: U of California P, 1994. Print.
Bluemel, Kristin. *Intermodernism: Literary Culture in Mid-Twentieth-Century Britain*. Edinburgh: Edinburgh UP, 2009. Print.
Boehmer, Elleke and Stephen Morton. *Terror and the Postcolonial*. Chichester: Wiley Blackwell, 2010. Print.
Booth, Allyson. *Postcards from the Trenches: Negotiating the Space between Modernism and the First World War*. New York: Oxford UP, 1996. Print.
Bourke, Joanna. *Dismembering the Male: Men's Bodies, Britain, and the Great War*. London: Reaktion, 1996. Print.
Bowen, Elizabeth. "The Demon Lover." *The Collected Stories of Elizabeth Bowen*. New York: Knopf, 1981. 661–6. Print.
Bowen, Elizabeth. "Mysterious Kôr." *The Collected Stories of Elizabeth Bowen*. New York: Knopf, 1981. 728–40. Print.
Bowen, Elizabeth. *The Heat of the Day*. London: Vintage, 1998. Print.
Bowen, Elizabeth. "Preface to *The Demon Lover*." *The Mulberry Tree; Writings of Elizabeth Bowen*. Ed. Hermione Lee. London: Viking, 1999. 5–8. Print.
Bowen, Elizabeth. *The Last September*. New York: Anchor, 2000. Print.
Bowen, Elizabeth. "Britain in Autumn." *People, Places, Things: Essays by Elizabeth Bowen*. Ed. Allan Hepburn. Edinburgh: Edinburgh UP, 2008. 48–55. Print.
Bowen, Elizabeth. "English Fiction at Mid-Century." *People, Places, Things: Essays by Elizabeth Bowen*. Ed. Allan Hepburn. Edinburgh: Edinburgh UP, 2008. 321–4. Print.
Bowen, Elizabeth. "The Idea of France." *People, Places, Things: Essays by Elizabeth Bowen*. Ed. Allan Hepburn. Edinburgh: Edinburgh UP, 2008. 61–5. Print.
Brearton, Fran. *The Great War in Irish Poetry: W. B. Yeats to Michael Longley*. Oxford: Oxford UP, 2000. Print.
Brooke, Rupert. "Peace." *The Poetical Works of Rupert Brooke*. Ed. Geoffrey Keynes. London: Faber, 1970. 19. Print.
Buch, Robert. *The Pathos of the Real: On the Aesthetics of Violence in the Twentieth Century*. Baltimore: Johns Hopkins UP, 2010. Print.
Calder, Angus. *The Myth of the Blitz*. Jonathan Cape: London, 1991. Print.
Campbell, James. "Combat Gnosticism: The Ideology of First World War Poetry Criticism." *New Literary History* 30.1 (1999): 203–15. Print.
Camus, Albert. *The Plague*. Trans. Robin Buss. London: Penguin, 2002. Print.
Cather, Willa. *One of Ours*. London: Virago, 1987. Print.
Céline, Louis-Ferdinand. *Journey to the End of the Night*. Trans. Ralph Manheim. New York: New Directions, 2006. Print.

Clewell, Tammy. *Modernism, Mourning, Postmodernism*. Basingstoke: Palgrave Macmillan, 2009. Print.
Clymer, Jeffory A. *America's Culture of Terrorism: Violence, Capitalism, and the Written Word*. Chapel Hill: U of North Carolina P, 2003. Print.
Cohen, Debra Rae. *Remapping the Home Front: Locating Citizenship in British Women's Great War Fiction*. Boston: Northeastern UP, 2002. Print.
Cole, Sarah. *Modernism, Male Friendship, and the First World War*. Cambridge: Cambridge UP, 2003. Print.
Cole, Sarah. *At the Violet Hour: Modernism and Violence in England and Ireland*. New York: Oxford UP, 2012. Print.
Connolly, Cyril. "Comment." *Horizon* 1.1 (1940): 5–6. Print.
Connolly, Cyril. "Comment." *Horizon* 1.2 (1940): 68–71. Print.
Connolly, Cyril. *Enemies of Promise*. Chicago: U of Chicago P, 2008. Print.
Conrad, Joseph. *Under Western Eyes*. London: Penguin, 2002. Print.
Conrad, Joseph. "Autocracy and War." *Notes on Life and Letters*. Ed. J. H. Stape. Cambridge: Cambridge UP, 2004. 71–93. Print.
Conrad, Joseph. *Heart of Darkness*. London: Penguin, 2007. Print.
Conrad, Joseph. "The Informer." *The Nigger of the "Narcissus" and Other Stories*. London: Penguin, 2007. 285–310. Print.
Conrad, Joseph. *The Secret Agent*. London: Penguin, 2007. Print.
Cooper, John Xiros. *T. S. Eliot and The Ideology of Four Quartets*. Cambridge: Cambridge UP, 1995. Print.
Cunard, Nancy. *Negro*. London: Nancy Cunard at Wishart & Co, 1934. Print.
Cunningham, Valentine. *British Writers of the Thirties*. Oxford: Oxford UP, 1988. Print.
Daly, Nicholas. *Modernism, Romance, and the Fin De Siècle: Popular Fiction and British Culture*. Cambridge: Cambridge UP, 1999. Print.
Darrohn, Christine. "'Blown to Bits!' Katherine Mansfield's 'The Garden Party' and The Great War." *Modern Fiction Studies* 44.3 (1998): 513–39. Print.
Davis, Thomas S. *The Extinct Scene: Late Modernism and Everyday Life*. New York: Columbia UP, 2015. Print.
Day Lewis, Cecil. "Letter to a Young Revolutionary." *New Country: Prose and Poetry by the Authors of "New Signatures."* Ed. Michael Roberts. London: Hogarth, 1933. 25–42. Print.
DeCoste, Damon Marcel. "Modernism's Shell-Shocked History: Amnesia, Repetition, and the War in Graham Greene's *The Ministry of Fear*." *Twentieth-Century Literature* 45.4 (1999): 428–51. Print.
Deer, Patrick. *Culture in Camouflage: War, Empire, and Modern British Literature*. New York: Oxford UP, 2009. Print.

Derrida, Jacques. "No Apocalypse, Not Now (Full Speed Ahead, Seven Missiles, Seven Missives)." Trans. Catherine Porter and Philip Lewis. *Diacritics* 14.2 (1984): 20–31. Print.
Douglas, Keith. "Poets in this War." *A Prose Miscellany*. Ed. Desmond Graham. Manchester: Carcanet, 1985. 117–20. Print.
Douglas, Keith. "Desert Flowers." *Complete Poems*. Ed. Desmond Graham. London: Faber, 1998. 108. Print.
Douglas, Keith. "*Vergissmeinnicht*." *Complete Poems*. Ed. Desmond Graham. London: Faber, 1998. 118. Print.
Douglas, Keith. *Alamein to Zem Zem*. London: Faber, 2008. Print.
Douhet, Guilio. *The Command of the Air*. Trans. Dino Ferrari. Tuscaloosa: U of Alabama P, 2009. Print.
Egremont, Max. *Siegfried Sassoon: A Biography*. London: Picador, 2005. Print.
Einhaus, Ann-Marie. *The Short Story and the First World War*. Cambridge: Cambridge UP, 2013. Print.
Eksteins, Modris. *Rites of Spring: The Great War and the Birth of the Modern Age*. London: Bantam, 1989. Print.
Eliot, T. S. *East Coker*. *Collected Poems, 1909–1962*. New York: Harcourt Brace, 1991. 182–90. Print.
Eliot, T. S. "Gerontion." *Collected Poems, 1909–1962*. New York: Harcourt Brace, 1991. 29–31. Print.
Eliot, T. S. *Little Gidding*. *Collected Poems, 1909–1962*. New York: Harcourt Brace, 1991. 200–9. Print.
Eliot, T. S. *The Waste Land*. *Collected Poems, 1909–1962*. New York: Harcourt Brace, 1991. 51–76. Print.
Eliot, T. S. "A Note of Introduction." David Jones, *In Parenthesis*. New York: New York Review Books Classics, 2003. vii–viii. Print.
Ellis, Steve. *The English Eliot: Design, Language and Landscape in "Four Quartets."* London: Routledge, 1991. Print.
Ellis, Steve. *British Writers and the Approach of World War II*. Cambridge: Cambridge UP, 2015. Print.
Ellmann, Maud. *The Poetics of Impersonality: T. S. Eliot and Ezra Pound*. Cambridge: Harvard UP, 1987. Print.
Eltis, Sos. *Revising Wilde: Society and Subversion in the Plays of Oscar Wilde*. Oxford: Clarendon, 1996. Print.
Empson, William. "Autumn on Nan-Yüeh." *Collected Poems*. London: Hogarth, 1984. 72–80. Print.
Esty, Jed. *A Shrinking Island: Modernism and National Culture in England*. Princeton: Princeton UP, 2004. Print.
Fitzgibbon, Constantine. *The Blitz*. London: Allan Wingate, 1957. Print.
Ford, Ford Madox. *The Good Soldier*. Oxford: Oxford UP, 2012. Print.
Ford, Ford Madox. *Parade's End*. London: Penguin, 2012. Print.

Foster, R. F. W. B. *Yeats: A Life, II: The Arch-Poet, 1915–39*. Oxford: Oxford UP, 2003. Print.
Freedman, Ariela. *Death, Men, and Modernism: Trauma and Narrative in British Fiction from Hardy to Woolf*. New York: Routledge, 2003. Print.
Freud, Sigmund. "On Transience." *The Standard Edition of the Complete Psychological Works of Sigmund Freud: Volume 14*. Trans. James Strachey. London: Hogarth, 1971. 307–9. Print.
Freud, Sigmund. "Thoughts for the Times on War and Death." *The Standard Edition of the Complete Psychological Works of Sigmund Freud: Volume 14*. Trans. James Strachey. London: Hogarth, 1971. 274–300. Print.
Fussell, Paul. *The Great War and Modern Memory*. New York: Oxford UP, 1975. Print.
Fussell, Paul. *Abroad: Literary Traveling Between the Wars*. New York: Oxford UP, 1980. Print.
Fussell, Paul. *Wartime: Understanding and Behavior in the Second World War*. New York: Oxford UP, 1989. Print.
Gandal, Keith. *The Gun and the Pen: Hemingway, Fitzgerald, Faulkner, and the Fiction of Mobilization*. New York: Oxford UP, 2008. Print.
Gibbon, Lewis Grassic. *Sunset Song*. London: Penguin, 2007. Print.
Grass, Günter. *The Tin Drum*. Trans. Ralph Manheim. New York: Vintage, 1990. Print.
Grausam, Daniel. *On Endings: American Postmodern Fiction in the Cold War*. Virginia: U of Virginia P, 2011. Print.
Green, Henry. *Caught*. London: Harvill, 1991. Print.
Green, Henry. *Party Going. Living/Loving/Party Going*. London: Penguin, 1993. 383–528. Print.
Green, Henry. *Pack My Bag*. New York: New Directions, 2004. Print.
Green, Henry. *Back*. Normal: Dalkey Archive P, 2009. Print.
Greene, Graham. *Stamboul Train*. London: Vintage, 2001. Print.
Greene, Graham. *The Ministry of Fear*. London: Penguin, 2005. Print.
Hara, Tamiki. "Summer Flower." Trans. George Saitō. *The Crazy Iris and Other Stories of the Atomic Aftermath*. Ed. Kenzaburo Ōe. New York: Grove, 1985. 37–54. Print.
Hardy, Thomas. "Channel Firing." *Selected Poems*. Ed. David Wright. Harmondsworth: Penguin, 1983. 258–9. Print.
Hardy, Thomas. "Drummer Hodge." *Selected Poems*. Ed. David Wright. Harmondsworth: Penguin, 1983. 257. Print.
Hardy, Thomas. "The Man He Killed." *Selected Poems*. Ed. David Wright. Harmondsworth: Penguin, 1983. 258–9. Print.
Hemingway, Ernest. "Soldier's Home." *In Our Time*. London: Jonathan Cape, 1926. 97–113. Print.

Hewison, Robert. *Under Siege: Literary Life in London, 1939–45*. London: Weidenfeld & Nicolson, 1977. Print.
Ho, Janice. *Nation and Citizenship in the Twentieth-Century British Novel*. New York: Cambridge UP, 2015. Print.
Hochschild, Adam. *To End All Wars: A Story of Loyalty and Rebellion, 1914–1918*. Boston: Houghton Mifflin Harcourt, 2011. Print.
Houen, Alex. *Terrorism and Modern Literature: From Joseph Conrad to Ciaran Carson*. Oxford: Oxford UP, 2002. Print.
Hynes, Samuel. *The Auden Generation*. London: Bodley Head, 1976. Print.
Hynes, Samuel. *A War Imagined: The First World War and English Culture*. London: Bodley Head, 1990. Print.
Isherwood, Christopher. *Goodbye to Berlin*. *The Berlin Novels*. London: Vintage, 1999. 237–490. Print.
Isherwood, Christopher. *Christopher and His Kind*. London: Vintage, 2012. Print.
James, Henry. *The Princess Casamassima*. Ed. Derek Brewer. London: Penguin, 1987.
James, Pearl. *The New Death: American Modernism and World War I*. Charlottesville: U of Virginia P, 2013. Print.
Jameson, Fredric. *The Seeds of Time*. New York: Columbia UP, 1994. Print.
Jameson, Fredric. *A Singular Modernity: Essay on the Ontology of the Present*. London: Verso, 2002. Print.
Jameson, Storm. *The Fort*. London: Cassell, 1941. Print.
Jeffery, Keith. *Ireland and the Great War*. Cambridge: Cambridge UP, 2000. Print.
Jeffery, Keith. "'Writing Out of Opinions': Irish Experience and the Theatre of the First World War." Ed. Santanu Das. *Race, Empire and First World War Writing*. Cambridge: Cambridge UP, 2011. 249–64. Print.
Jones, David. *In Parenthesis*. New York: New York Rev. of Books Classics, 2003. Print.
Jordan, Heather Bryant. *How Will the Heart Endure: Elizabeth Bowen and the Landscapes of War*. Ann Arbor: U of Michigan P, 1992. Print.
Kaplan, Carola M., Peter Lancelot Mallios, and Andrea White, Eds. *Conrad in the Twenty-First Century: Contemporary Approaches and Perspectives*. New York: Routledge, 2005. Print.
Kendall, Tim. *Modern English War Poetry*. Oxford: Oxford UP, 2006. Print.
Keyes, Sydney. "Meditation of Phlebas the Phoenician." *Collected Poems*. Manchester: Carcanet, 2002. 104. Print.
Kiberd, Declan. *Inventing Ireland: The Literature of the Modern Nation*. Cambridge: Harvard UP, 1995. Print.
Kipling, Rudyard. "Epitaphs of the War." *War Stories and Poems*. Ed. Andrew Rutherford. Oxford: Oxford UP, 1999. 321–4. Print.

Kipling, Rudyard. "The Gardener." *War Stories and Poems*. Ed. Andrew Rutherford. Oxford: Oxford UP, 1999. 310–20. Print.
Kipling, Rudyard. "Mary Postgate." *War Stories and Poems*. Ed. Andrew Rutherford. Oxford: Oxford UP, 1999. 235–49. Print.
Kipling, Rudyard. "The Widow's Party." *War Stories and Poems*. Ed. Andrew Rutherford. Oxford: Oxford UP, 1999. 5–6. Print.
Knowles, Sebastian D. G. *A Purgatorial Flame: Seven British Writers in the Second World War*. Philadelphia: U of Pennsylvania P, 1990. Print.
Kohlmann, Benjamin. *Committed Styles: Modernism, Politics, and Left-Wing Literature in the 1930s*. Oxford: Oxford UP, 2014. Print.
Larkin, Philip. "Homage to a Government." *Collected Poems*. Ed. Anthony Thwaite. London: Faber & Faber and the Marvell P, 1989. 171. Print.
Lassner, Phyllis. *British Women Writers of World War II: Battlegrounds of Their Own*. Basingstoke: Macmillan, 1998. Print.
Lawrence, D. H. "The Prussian Officer." *The Prussian Officer and Other Stories*. Oxford: Oxford UP, 1995. 200–22. Print.
Lawrence, D. H. "The Shadow in the Rose Garden." *The Prussian Officer and Other Stories*. Oxford: Oxford UP, 1995. 126–39. Print.
Lawrence, D. H. "The Thorn in the Flesh." *The Prussian Officer and Other Stories*. Oxford: Oxford UP, 1995. 180–99. Print.
Lawrence, D. H. *Lady Chatterley's Lover*. New York: Modern Library, 2001. Print.
Lee, Stephen J. *The European Dictatorships 1918–1945*. London: Routledge, 1998. Print.
Leed, Eric. *No Man's Land: Combat and Identity in World War I*. New York: Cambridge UP, 1979. Print.
Lehmann, John. *New Writing in Europe*. Harmondsworth: Penguin, 1940. Print.
Levenback, Karen L. *Virginia Woolf and the Great War*. Syracuse: Syracuse UP, 1999. Print.
Lewis, Pericles. "Inventing Literary Modernism at the Outbreak of the Great War." Ed. Michael J. K. Walsh. Cambridge: Cambridge UP, 2010. 148–64. Print.
Lewis, Wyndham. "Long Live the Vortex!" *BLAST*. No. 1. (June 1914): NP. Print.
Lewis, Wyndham. "Editorial." *BLAST*. No. 2. (July 1915): 5–6. Print.
Lewis, Wyndham. *Blasting and Bombardiering: An Autobiography, 1914–1926*. London: John Calder, 1982. Print.
Liddell, Robert. *Unreal City*. London: Jonathan Cape, 1952. Print.
Lifton, Robert Jay. *Death in Life: Survivors of Hiroshima*. Chapel Hill: U of North Carolina P, 1991. Print.

Macaulay, Rose. *The World My Wilderness*. London: The Book Club, 1949. Print.
Maclean, Caroline. *The Vogue for Russia: Modernism and the Unseen in Britain, 1900–1930*. Edinburgh: Edinburgh UP, 2015. Print.
MacLean, Sorley. "Death Valley." *From Wood to Ridge: Collected Poems*. Manchester and Edinburgh: Carcanet and Birlinn, 1999. 201–13. Print.
MacNeice, Louis. "Brother Fire." *Collected Poems*. Ed. E. R. Dodds. London: Faber, 2007. 196. Print
Mallios, Peter Lancelot. "Reading *The Secret Agent* Now: The Press, the Police, the Premonition of Simulation." *Conrad in the Twenty-First Century: Contemporary Approaches and Perspectives*. New York: Routledge, 2005. 155–72. Print.
Mansfield, Katherine. *Journal of Katherine Mansfield*. Ed. J. Middleton Murry. London: Constable, 1954. Print.
Mansfield, Katherine. "The Fly." *Stories*. New York: Vintage, 1991. 343–8. Print.
Mansfield, Katherine. "The Garden Party." *Stories*. New York: Vintage, 1991. 282–97. Print.
Mansfield, Katherine. *The Collected Letters of Katherine Mansfield: Volume 3*. Ed. Vincent O'Sullivan and Margaret Scott. Oxford: Oxford UP, 1993. Print.
Marcus, Laura. "'The Creative Treatment of Actuality': John Grierson, Documentary Cinema and 'Fact' in the 1930s." *Intermodernism: Literary Culture in Mid-Twentieth-Century Britain*. Ed. Kristin Bluemel. Edinburgh: Edinburgh UP, 2011. 189–207. Print.
Marinetti, Filippo. "The Founding and Manifesto of Futurism." *Selected Writings*. Ed. R. W. Flint. Trans. R. W. Flint and Arthur A. Coppotelli. London: Secker & Warburg, 1972. 39–44. Print.
Marx, John. *The Modernist Novel and the Decline of Empire*. Cambridge: Cambridge UP, 2005. Print.
May, Philip. *Love, the Reward*. London: Remington, 1885. Print.
McClure, John A. *Late Imperial Romance*. London: Verso, 1994. Print.
McHale, Brian. *Postmodernist Fiction*. London: Routledge, 2001. Print.
McNulty, Eugene. "Incommensurate Histories: The Remaindered Irish Bodies of the Great War." *Conflict, Nationhood and Corporeality in Modern Literature: Bodies-At-War*. Ed. Petra Rau. Basingstoke: Palgrave Macmillan, 2010. 64–82. Print.
Melchiori, Barbara Arnett. *Terrorism in the Late Victorian Novel*. London: Croom Helm, 1985. Print.
Mellor, Leo. *Reading the Ruins: Modernism, Bombsites and British Culture*. Cambridge: Cambridge UP, 2011. Print.
Middleton, Peter. "The Masculinity Behind the Ghosts of Modernism in Eliot's *Four Quartets*." *Gender, Desire, and Sexuality in T. S. Eliot*. Ed.

Cassandra Laity and Nancy K. Gish. Cambridge: Cambridge UP, 2004. 83–104. Print.

Miller, Kristine A. *British Literature of the Blitz: Fighting the People's War*. Basingstoke: Palgrave Macmillan, 2009. Print.

Miller, Tyrus. *Late Modernism: Politics, Fiction, and the Arts between the World Wars*. Berkeley: U of California P, 1999. Print.

Miller, Tyrus. "Documentary/Modernism: Convergence and Complementarity in the 1930s." *Modernism/modernity* 9.2 (2002): 226–41. Print.

Mitchell, J. Lawrence. "Katherine Mansfield's War." *Katherine Mansfield Studies* 6 (2014): 27–41. Print.

Moore, George. *A Drama in Muslin*. London: Vizetelly, 1886. Print.

Musil, Robert. *The Man Without Qualities*, Trans. Sophie Wilkins and Burton Pike. London: Picador, 2011. Print.

Nabokov, Vladimir. "Signs and Symbols." *Nabokov's Dozen: A Collection of Thirteen Stories*. Garden City: Doubleday, 1958. 67–74. Print.

Newton, Michael. "'Nihilists of Castlebar!' Exporting Russian Nihilism in the 1880s and the Case of Oscar Wilde's *Vera; or the Nihilists*." *Russia in Britain, 1880–1940: From Melodrama to Modernism*. Ed. Rebecca Beasley and Philip Ross Bullock. Oxford: Oxford UP, 2013. 35–52. Print.

Nichols, Bill. "Documentary Film and the Modernist Avant-Garde." *Critical Inquiry* 27.4 (2001): 580–610. Print.

Norris, Margot. *Writing War in the Twentieth Century*. Charlottesville: U of Virginia P, 2000. Print.

North, Michael. *Henry Green and the Writing of His Generation*. Charlottesville: U of Virginia P, 1984. Print.

North, Michael. *Reading 1922: A Return to the Scene of the Modern*. Oxford: Oxford UP, 1999. Print.

O'Casey, Sean. *Juno and the Paycock*. Plays 1. London: Faber, 1998. 1–86. Print.

O'Casey, Sean. *The Plough and the Stars*. Plays 2. London: Faber, 1998. 63–161. Print.

O'Casey, Sean. *The Shadow of a Gunman*. Plays 2. London: Faber, 1998. 1–62. Print.

O'Casey, Sean. *The Silver Tassie*. Plays 2. London: Faber, 1998. 163–269. Print.

Ó Donghaile, Deaglán. *Blasted Literature: Victorian Political Fiction and the Shock of Modernism*. Edinburgh: Edinburgh UP, 2011. Print.

Orwell, George. *Coming Up For Air*. San Diego: Harcourt, 1950. Print.

Orwell, George. "Looking Back on the Spanish War." *The Collected Essays, Journalism, and Letters of George Orwell: Vol 2: My Country Right or Left, 1940–43*. Ed. Sonia Orwell and Ian Angus. London: Secker & Warburg, 1968. 249–67. Print.

Orwell, George. "Spilling the Spanish Beans." *The Collected Essays, Journalism, and Letters of George Orwell: Vol 2: My Country Right or Left, 1940–43*. Ed. Sonia Orwell and Ian Angus. London: Secker & Warburg, 1968. 269–76. Print.

Orwell, George. "Inside the Whale." *A Collection of Essays*. Orlando: Harcourt, 1981. 210–52. Print.

Orwell, George. "Why I Write." *A Collection of Essays*. Orlando: Harcourt, 1981. 309–16. Print.

Orwell, George. *Homage to Catalonia*. London: Penguin, 2013. Print.

Ouditt, Sharon. *Fighting Forces, Writing Women*. New York: Routledge, 1994. Print.

Outka, Elizabeth. "'Wood for the Coffins Ran Out': Modernism and the Shadowed Afterlife of the Influenza Pandemic." *Modernism/modernity* 21.4 (2015): 937–60. Print.

Owen, Wilfred. "Dulce et Decorum Est." *The War Poems of Wilfred Owen*. Ed. Jon Stallworthy. London: Chatto & Windus, 1994. 29–30. Print.

Owen, Wilfred. "Owen's Preface." *The War Poems of Wilfred Owen*. Ed. Jon Stallworthy. London: Chatto & Windus, 1994. 98. Print.

Owen, Wilfred. "The Parable of the Old Man and the Young." *The War Poems of Wilfred Owen*. Ed. Jon Stallworthy. London: Chatto & Windus, 1994. 61. Print.

Owen, Wilfred. "Strange Meeting." *The War Poems of Wilfred Owen*. Ed. Jon Stallworthy. London: Chatto & Windus, 1994. 35–7. Print.

Parker, Peter. *Isherwood: A Life*. London: Picador, 2005. Print.

Parkes, Adam. *A Sense of Shock: The Impact of Impressionism on Modern British and Irish Writing*. Oxford: Oxford UP, 2011. Print.

Piette, Adam. *Imagination at War: British Fiction and Poetry 1939–1945*. London: Papermac, 1995. Print.

Plain, Gill. *Women's Fiction of the Second World War: Gender, Power and Resistance*. Edinburgh: Edinburgh UP, 1996. Print.

Pound, Ezra. *The Pisan Cantos*. Ed. Richard Sieburth. New York: New Directions, 2003. Print.

Pound, Ezra. *Hugh Selwyn Mauberley*. *New Selected Poems and Translations*. Ed. Richard Sieburth. New York: New Directions, 2010. 109–23. Print.

Powell, Anthony. *The Acceptance World*. *A Dance to the Music of Time: First Movement*. Chicago: U of Chicago P, 1995. Print.

Powell, Anthony. *At Lady Molly's*. *A Dance to the Music of Time: Second Movement*. Chicago: U of Chicago P, 1995. Print.

Powell, Anthony. *The Military Philosophers*. *A Dance to the Music of Time: Third Movement*. Chicago: U of Chicago P, 1995. Print.

Puchner, Martin. *Poetry of the Revolution: Marx, Manifestos, and the Avant-Gardes*. Princeton: Princeton UP, 2005. Print.

Rae, Patricia, Ed. *Modernism and Mourning*. Lewisburg: Bucknell UP, 2007. Print.
Raitt, Suzanne and Trudi Tate. *Women's Fiction and the Great War*. Oxford: Clarendon, 1997. Print.
Rau, Petra. "Introduction: Between Absence and Ubiquity—On the Meanings of the Body-at-War." *Conflict, Nationhood and Corporeality in Modern Literature: Bodies-at-War*. Ed. Petra Rau. Basingstoke: Palgrave Macmillan, 2010. 1–25. Print.
Rawlinson, Mark. *British Writing of the Second World War*. Oxford: Clarendon, 2000. Print.
Read, Herbert. *In Retreat*. London: Imperial War Museum, 1991. Print.
Reed, John. *Ten Days That Shook the World*. London: Lawrence & Wishart, 1961. Print.
Rogers, Gayle. *Modernism and the New Spain: Britain, Cosmopolitan Europe, and Literary History*. New York: Oxford UP, 2012. Print.
Rosenberg, Isaac. "Break of Day in the Trenches." *Poetry of the First World War: An Anthology*. Ed. Tim Kendall. Oxford: Oxford UP, 2013. 137–8. Print.
Roth, Joseph. *The Radetzky March*. Trans. Michael Hofmann. London: Granta, 2003. Print.
Saint-Amour, Paul K. *Tense Future: Modernism, Total War, Encyclopedic Form*. New York: Oxford UP, 2015. Print.
Sansom, William. "Fireman Flower." *Fireman Flower and Other Stories*. London: Hogarth, 1944. 126–63. Print.
Sassoon, Siegfried. "Blighters." *Collected Poems 1908–56*. London: Faber, 1956. 21. Print.
Sassoon, Siegfried. "The Fathers." *Collected Poems 1908–56*. London: Faber, 1956. 74–5. Print.
Scanlan, Margaret. *Plotting Terror: Novelists and Terrorists in Contemporary Fiction*. Charlottesville: U of Virginia P, 2001. Print.
Scarry, Elaine. *The Body in Pain: The Making and Unmaking of the World*. New York: Oxford UP, 1985.
Schweitzer, Bernard. *Radicals on the Road: The Politics of English Travel Writing in the 1930s*. Charlottesville: U of Virginia P, 2001. Print.
Seiler, Claire. "At Midcentury: Elizabeth Bowen's *The Heat of the Day*." *Modernism/modernity* 21.1 (2014): 125–45. Print.
Shaw, George Bernard. *Heartbreak House: A Fantasia in the Russian Manner on English Themes*. London: Longmans, Green, 1961. Print.
Shaw, George Bernard. *Arms and the Man*. London: Methuen, 2008. Print.
Sherman, David. *In a Strange Room: Modernism's Corpses and Mortal Obligation*. Oxford: Oxford UP, 2014. Print.
Sherry, Vincent. *The Great War and the Language of Modernism*. New York: Oxford UP, 2003. Print.

Sherry, Vincent. "The Great War and Literary Modernism in England." *The Cambridge Companion to the Literature of the First World War*. Ed. Vincent Sherry. Cambridge: Cambridge UP, 2005. 113–37. Print.

Showalter, Elaine. *The Female Malady: Women, Madness, and English Culture, 1830–1980*. London: Virago, 1987. Print.

Sillars, Stuart. *British Romantic Art and the Second World War*. Basingstoke: Macmillan, 1991. Print.

Smith, Angela K. *Women's Writing of the First World War*. Manchester: Manchester UP, 2000. Print.

Sontag, Susan. *Regarding the Pain of Others*. New York: Picador, 2003. Print.

Sorley, Charles. "When You See Millions of the Mouthless Dead." *Poetry of the First World War: An Anthology*. Ed. Tim Kendall. Oxford: Oxford UP, 2013. 191. Print.

Stansky, Peter. *The First Day of the Blitz*. New Haven: Yale UP, 2007. Print.

Stevenson, Robert Louis. *The Dynamiter*. New York: Henry Holt, 1885. Print.

Stites, Richard. *Revolutionary Dreams: Utopian Vision and Experimental Life in the Russian Revolution*. New York: Oxford UP, 1988. Print.

Stonebridge, Lyndsey. *The Writing of Anxiety: Imagining Wartime in Mid-Century British Culture*. Basingstoke: Palgrave Macmillan, 2007. Print.

Synge, J. M. *The Playboy of the Western World and Other Plays*. Oxford: Oxford UP, 2008. Print.

Tate, Trudi. *Modernism, History and the First World War*. Manchester: Manchester UP, 1996. Print.

Taylor, Antony. *London's Burning: Pulp Fiction, the Politics of Terrorism and the Destruction of the Capital in British Popular Culture, 1840–2005*. London: Continuum, 2012. Print.

Thomas, Dylan. *The Collected Letters*. Ed. Paul Ferris. London: Dent, 1985. Print.

Treglown, Jeremy. *Romancing: The Life and Work of Henry Green*. New York: Random House, 2000. Print.

Walsh, Michael J. K. *London, Modernism, and 1914*. Cambridge: Cambridge UP, 2010. Print.

Watt, Ian. *Conrad in the Nineteenth Century*. Berkeley: U of California P, 1981. Print.

Waugh, Evelyn. *Put Out More Flags*. Boston: Back Bay, 1970. Print.

Waugh, Evelyn. "Two Unquiet Lives." Ed. Donat Gallagher. *The Essays, Articles and Reviews of Evelyn Waugh*. London: Methuen, 1983. 394–8. Print.

Waugh, Evelyn. *Sword of Honour*. New York: Knopf, 1994. Print.

Waugh, Evelyn. *Scoop*. Boston: Back Bay, 1999. Print.

Waugh, Evelyn. *Black Mischief*. Boston: Back Bay, 2002. Print.

Wells, H. G. *Mr Britling Sees it Through*. London: Cassell, 1916. Print.
Wells, H. G. *The Island of Dr Moreau*. Harmondsworth: Penguin, 1946. Print.
Wells, H. G. *The Time Machine*. London: Penguin, 2005. Print.
Wells, H. G. *The War of the Worlds*. London: Gollancz, 2012. Print.
West, Rebecca. *Black Lamb and Grey Falcon: A Journey Through Yugoslavia*. Edinburgh: Canongate, 1993. Print.
West, Rebecca. *The Return of the Soldier*. London: Penguin, 1998. Print.
Whittier-Ferguson, John. *Mortality and Form in Late Modernist Literature*. Cambridge: Cambridge UP, 2014. Print.
Wilde, Oscar. *Vera, or the Nihilists*. London: Methuen, 1927. Print.
Will, Barbara. *Unlikely Collaboration: Gertrude Stein, Bernard Faÿ, and the Vichy Dilemma*. New York: Columbia UP, 2011. Print.
Winter, Jay. *Sites of Memory, Sites of Mourning: The Great War in European Cultural History*. Cambridge: Cambridge UP, 2005. Print.
Wollaeger, Mark. *Modernism, Media, and Propaganda: British Narrative from 1900 to 1945*. Princeton: Princeton UP, 2006. Print.
Wood, Michael. *Yeats and Violence*. Oxford: Oxford UP, 2010. Print.
Woolf, Virginia. "The Leaning Tower." *The Moment and Other Essays*. London: Hogarth, 1947. 105–25. Print.
Woolf, Virginia. *Three Guineas*. Harmondsworth: Penguin, 1977. Print.
Woolf, Virginia. *The Diary of Virginia Woolf: Volume Two; 1920–1924*. Ed. Anne Olivier Bell, with Andrew McNeillie. New York: Harcourt Brace, 1978. Print.
Woolf, Virginia. *To the Lighthouse: The Original Holograph Draft*. Ed. Susan Dick. London: Hogarth, 1983. Appendix A. 43–50. Print.
Woolf, Virginia. "Modern Fiction." *The Virginia Woolf Reader*. Ed. Mitchell A. Leaska. San Diego: Harcourt, 1984. 283–91. Print.
Woolf, Virginia. *A Moment's Liberty: The Shorter Diary of Virginia Woolf*. Ed. Anne Olivier Bell. San Diego: Harcourt, 1990. Print.
Woolf, Virginia. *Mrs Dalloway*. Oxford: Oxford UP, 1992. Print.
Woolf, Virginia. *To the Lighthouse*. Oxford: Oxford UP, 1992. Print.
Woolf, Virginia. *Jacob's Room*. Oxford: Oxford UP, 1999. Print.
Woolf, Virginia. *A Room of One's Own*. London: Penguin, 2002. Print.
Woolf, Virginia. "Memoir of Julian Bell." Ed. S. P. Rosenbaum. *The Platform of Time: Memoirs of Family and Friends*. London: Hesperus, 2007. 19–32. Print.
Woolf, Virginia. *Between the Acts*. Orlando: Harcourt, 2008. Print.
Woolf, Virginia. *The Years*. Orlando: Harcourt, 2008. Print.
Yeats, W. B. "Easter 1916." *Collected Poems*. London: Picador, 1995. 202–5. Print.
Yeats, W. B. "An Irish Airman Foresees His Death." *Collected Poems*. London: Picador, 1995. 152. Print.

Yeats, W. B. "The Man and the Echo." *Collected Poems*. London: Picador, 1995. 393–5. Print.

Yeats, W. B. "Meditations in Time of Civil War." *Collected Poems*. London: Picador, 1995. 225–32. Print.

Yeats, W. B. "Nineteen Hundred and Nineteen." *Collected Poems*. London: Picador, 1995. 232–7. Print.

Yeats, W. B. "On Being Asked for a War Poem." *Collected Poems*. London: Picador, 1995. 175. Print.

Yeats, W. B. "The Rose Tree." *Collected Poems*. London: Picador, 1995. 206. Print.

Yeats, W. B. "Sixteen Dead Men." *Collected Poems*. London: Picador, 1995. 205. Print.

Yeats, W. B. "J. M. Synge and the Ireland of His Time." *The Collected Works of W. B. Yeats, Vol. IV*. Ed. George Bornstein and Richard J. Finneran. New York: Scribner, 2007. 226–47. Print.

BIBLIOGRAPHY

1 A terrible beauty is born

Brantlinger, Patrick. *Rule of Darkness: British Literature and Imperialism, 1830–1914.* Ithaca: Cornell UP, 1988.
Clarke, I. F. *Voices Prophesying War: Future Wars, 1763–3749.* Oxford: Oxford UP, 1992.
Cole, Sarah. *At the Violet Hour: Modernism and Violence in England and Ireland.* New York: Oxford UP, 2012.
Daly, Nicholas. *Modernism, Romance, and the Fin de Siècle: Popular Fiction and British Culture, 1880–1914.* Cambridge: Cambridge UP, 1999.
Howlett, Jana and Rod Mengham. *The Violent Muse: Violence and the Artistic Imagination in Europe, 1910–1939.* Manchester: Manchester UP, 1994.
Kendall, Tim. *Modern English War Poetry.* Oxford: Oxford UP, 2006.
Lycett, Andrew. *Kipling and War: From "Tommy" to "My Boy Jack."* London: I. B. Tauris, 2015.
McLoughlin, Kate. *Authoring War: The Literary Representation of War from the Iliad to Iraq.* Cambridge: Cambridge UP, 2011.
Perloff, Marjorie. *The Futurist Moment: Avant-Garde, Avant Guerre, and the Language of Rupture.* Chicago: U of Chicago P, 1986.

2 Modernism and the Great War

Bergonzi, Bernard. *Heroes' Twilight: A Study of the Literature of the Great War.* Third Edition. Manchester: Carcanet, 1996.
Bonikowski, Wyatt. *Shell Shock and the Modernist Imagination: The Death Drive in Post-World War I British Fiction.* Burlington: Ashgate, 2013.
Booth, Allyson. *Postcards from the Trenches: Negotiating the Space between Modernism and the First World War.* New York: Oxford UP, 1996.
Buck, Claire. *Conceiving Strangeness in British First World War Writing.* Basingstoke: Palgrave Macmillan, 2015.

Caesar, Adrian. *Taking It Like a Man: Suffering, Sexuality and the War Poets*. Manchester: Manchester UP, 1993.
Cobley, Evelyn. *Representing War: Form and Ideology in First World War Narratives*. Toronto: U of Toronto P, 1993.
Cole, Sarah. *Modernism, Male Friendship, and the First World War*. Cambridge: Cambridge UP, 2003.
Das, Santanu. *Touch and Intimacy in First World War Writing*. Cambridge: Cambridge UP 2005.
Das, Santanu. *Race, Empire and First World War Writing*. Cambridge: Cambridge UP, 2011.
Dawes, James. *The Language of War: Literature and Culture in the U.S. from the Civil War through World War II*. Cambridge: Harvard UP, 2002.
Dodman, Trevor. *Shell Shock, Memory, and the Novel in the Wake of World War I*. New York: Cambridge UP, 2015.
Eksteins, Modris. *Rites of Spring: The Great War and the Birth of the Modern Age*. Boston: Houghton Mifflin, 1989.
Froula, Christine. *Virginia Woolf and the Bloomsbury Avant-Garde: War, Civilization, Modernity*. New York: Columbia UP, 2005.
Fussell, Paul. *The Great War and Modern Memory*. New York: Oxford UP, 1975.
Gilbert, Sandra. "'Rat's Alley': The Great War, Modernism, and the (Anti) Pastoral Elegy," *New Literary History* 30.1 (1999): 179–201.
Gilbert, Sandra M. and Susan Gubar. *No Man's Land: The Place of the Woman Writer in the Twentieth Century, Volume II: Sexchanges*. New Haven: Yale UP, 1989.
Haslam, Sara. *Fragmenting Modernism: Ford Madox Ford, the Novel, and the Great War*. Manchester: Manchester UP, 2002.
Hynes, Samuel. *A War Imagined: The First World War and English Culture*. London: Bodley Head, 1990.
Jackson, Paul. *Great War Modernisms and "The New Age" Magazine*. London: Continuum, 2012.
Khan, Nosheen. *Women's Poetry of the First World War*. London: Harvester Wheatsheaf, 1988.
Krockel, Carl. *War Trauma and English Modernism: T. S. Eliot and D. H. Lawrence*. Basingstoke: Palgrave Macmillan, 2011.
Larabee, Mark D. *Front Lines of Modernism: Remapping the Great War in British Fiction*. New York: Palgrave Macmillan, 2011.
Norris, Margot. *Writing War in the Twentieth Century*. Charlottesville: U of Virginia P, 2000.
Potter, Jane. *Boys in Khaki, Girls in Print: Women's Literary Responses to the Great War*. Oxford: Oxford UP, 2005.

Quinn, Patrick J. and Steven Trout. *The Literature of the Great War Reconsidered: Beyond Modern Memory*. Basingstoke: Palgrave, 2001.
Raitt, Suzanne and Trudi Tate. *Women's Fiction and the Great War*. Oxford: Clarendon, 1997.
Sherry, Vincent. *The Great War and the Language of Modernism*. New York: Oxford UP, 2003.
Sherry, Vincent. *The Cambridge Companion to the Literature of the First World War*. Cambridge: Cambridge UP, 2005.
Smith, Angela K. *The Second Battlefield: Women, Modernism, and the First World War*. Manchester: Manchester UP, 2000.
Stevenson, Randall. *Literature and the Great War, 1914–1918*. Oxford: Oxford UP, 2013.
Tate, Trudi. *Modernism, History and the First World War*. Manchester: Manchester UP, 1998.
Tylee, Claire. *The Great War and Women's Consciousness: Images of Militarism and Feminism in Women's Writings, 1914–64*. Basingstoke: Macmillan, 1990.
Walsh, Michael K. *London, Modernism, and 1914*. Cambridge: Cambridge UP, 2010.
Winter, Jay. *Sites of Memory, Sites of Mourning: The Great War in European Cultural History*. Cambridge: Cambridge UP, 1995.

3 Modernism and political violence

Allen, Nicholas. *Modernism, Ireland and Civil War*. Cambridge: Cambridge UP, 2009.
Brearton, Fran. *The Great War in Irish Poetry: W. B. Yeats to Michael Longley*. Oxford: Oxford UP, 2000.
Buch, Robert. *The Pathos of the Real: On the Aesthetics of Violence in the Twentieth Century*. Baltimore: Johns Hopkins UP, 2010.
Caws, Mary Ann, ed. *Manifesto: A Century of Isms*. Lincoln: U of Nebraska P, 2001.
Clymer, Jeffory A. *America's Culture of Terrorism: Violence, Capitalism, and the Written Word*. Chapel Hill: U of North Carolina P, 2003.
Cole, Sarah. *At the Violet Hour: Modernism and Violence in England and Ireland*. New York: Oxford UP, 2012.
Cullingford, Elizabeth. *Yeats, Ireland and Fascism*. New York: New York UP, 1981.
Haughey, Jim. *The First World War in Irish Poetry*. Lewisburg: Bucknell UP, 2002.

Houen, Alex. *Terrorism and Modern Literature from Joseph Conrad to Ciaran Carson*. Oxford: Oxford UP, 2002.
Kiberd, Declan. *Inventing Ireland: The Literature of the Modern Nation*. Cambridge: Harvard UP, 1995.
Lyon, Janet. *Manifestoes: Provocations of the Modern*. Ithaca: Cornell UP, 1999.
Melchiori, Barbara Arnett. *Terrorism in the Late Victorian Novel*. London: Croom Helm, 1985.
Ó Donghaile, Deaglán. *Blasted Literature: Victorian Political Fiction and the Shock of Modernism*. Edinburgh: Edinburgh UP, 2011.
Puchner, Martin. *Poetry of the Revolution: Marx, Manifestos, and the Avant-Gardes*. Princeton: Princeton UP, 2005.
Scanlan, Margaret. *Plotting Terror: Novelists and Terrorists in Contemporary Fiction*. Charlottesville: U of Virginia P, 2001.

4 Journeys to a war

Berman, Jessica. *Modernist Commitments: Ethics, Politics, and Transnational Modernism*. New York: Columbia UP, 2011.
Bluemel, Kristin. *Intermodernism: Literary Culture in Mid-Twentieth-Century Britain*. Edinburgh: Edinburgh UP, 2009.
Bryant, Marsha. *Auden and Documentary in the 1930s*. Charlottesville: U of Virginia P, 1997.
Cunningham, Valentine. *British Writers of the Thirties*. Oxford: Oxford UP, 1988.
Davis, Thomas S. *The Extinct Scene: Late Modernism and Everyday Life*. New York: Columbia UP, 2015.
Farley, David G. *Modernist Travel Writing: Intellectuals Abroad*. Columbia: U of Missouri P, 2010.
Fussell, Paul. *Abroad: British Literary Traveling between the Wars*. New York: Oxford UP, 1980.
Hynes, Samuel. *The Auden Generation: Literature and Politics in England in the 1930s*. London: Bodley Head, 1976.
Montefiore, Janet. *Men and Women Writers of the 1930s: The Dangerous Flood of History*. London: Routledge, 1996.
Patterson, Ian. *Guernica and Total War*. Cambridge: Harvard UP, 2007.
Rogers, Gayle. *Modernism and the New Spain: Britain, Cosmopolitan Europe, and Literary History*. New York: Oxford UP, 2012.
Schweitzer, Bernard. *Radicals on the Road: The Politics of English Travel Writing in the 1930s*. Charlottesville: U of Virginia P, 2001.

5 Modernism and the Second World War

Alldritt, Keith. *Modernism in the Second World War: The Later Poetry of Ezra Pound, T. S. Eliot, Basil Bunting, and Hugh MacDiarmid.* New York: Peter Lang, 1989.
Beer, Gillian. "The Island and the Aeroplane: The Case of Virginia Woolf." *Nation and Narration.* Ed. Homi K. Bhabha. London: Routledge, 1990. 265–90.
Deer, Patrick. *Culture in Camouflage: War, Empire, and Modern British Literature.* New York: Oxford UP, 2009.
Ellis, Steve. *British Writers and the Approach of World War II.* Cambridge: Cambridge UP, 2015.
Fussell, Paul. *Wartime: Understanding and Behavior in the Second World War.* New York: Oxford UP, 1989.
Knowles, Sebastian D. G. *A Purgatorial Flame: Seven British Writers in the Second World War.* Philadelphia: U of Pennsylvania P, 1990.
Lassner, Phyllis. *British Women Writers of World War II: Battlegrounds of their Own.* London: Macmillan, 1998.
MacKay, Marina. *Modernism and World War II.* Cambridge: Cambridge UP, 2007.
MacKay, Marina. *The Cambridge Companion to the Literature of World War II.* Cambridge: Cambridge UP, 2009.
Mellor, Leo. *Reading the Ruins: Modernism, Bombsites and British Culture.* Cambridge: Cambridge UP, 2011.
Miller, Kristine A. *British Literature of the Blitz: Fighting the People's War.* Basingstoke: Palgrave, 2009.
Miller, Tyrus. "Documentary/Modernism: Convergence and Complementarity in the 1930s." *Modernism/modernity* 9.2 (2002): 226–41.
Piette, Adam. *Imagination at War: British Fiction and Poetry 1939–1945.* Basingstoke: Papermac, 2005.
Plain, Gill. *Women's Fiction of the Second World War: Gender, Power, and Resistance.* Edinburgh: Edinburgh UP, 1996.
Rawlinson, Mark. *British Writing of the Second World War.* Oxford: Oxford UP, 2000.
Schneider, Karen. *Loving Arms: British Women Writing the Second World War.* Lexington: UP of Kentucky, 1997.
Stonebridge, Lyndsey. *The Writing of Anxiety: Imagining Wartime in Mid-Century British Culture.* Basingstoke: Palgrave Macmillan, 2007.
Whittier-Ferguson, John. *Mortality and Form in Late Modernist Literature.* New York: Cambridge UP, 2014.
Woodward, Guy. *Culture, Northern Ireland, and the Second World War.* Oxford: Oxford UP, 2015.

Epilogue: Cold War modernism?

Barnhisel, Greg. *Cold War Modernists: Art, Literature, and American Cultural Diplomacy*. New York: Columbia UP, 2015.

Genter, Robert. *Late Modernism: Art, Culture, and Politics in Cold War America*. Philadelphia: U of Pennsylvania P, 2010.

Mieszkowski, Jan. "Great War, Cold War, Total War." *Modernism/modernity* 16.2 (2009): 211–28.

Miller, Tyrus. *Late Modernism: Politics, Fiction, and the Arts between the World Wars*. Berkeley: U of California P, 1999.

Saint-Amour, Paul. *Tense Future: Modernism, Total War, Encyclopedic Form*. New York: Oxford UP, 2015.

Schwenger, Peter. *Letter Bomb: Nuclear Holocaust and the Exploding Word*. Baltimore: The Johns Hopkins UP, 1992.

Smith, James. *British Writers and MI5 Surveillance, 1930–1960*. Cambridge: Cambridge UP, 2013.

Stonor Saunders, Frances. *The Cultural Cold War: The C.I.A. and the World of Arts and Letters*. New York: New P, 2000.

Végsö, Roland. *The Naked Communist: Cold War Modernism and the Politics of Popular Culture*. New York: Fordham UP, 2013.

INDEX

9/11 terrorist attack 62, 64, 66

A Dance to the Music of Time (1951–75) 99–100, 129
A Drama in Muslin (1886) 81
A Genealogy of Modernism (1984) 130
A Purgatorial Flame 119
A Room of One's Own (1929) 59–60
A Sense of Shock (2011) 67, 70
A Singular Modernity (2002) 132
A War Imagined: The First World War and English Culture (1990) 23, 45–6
Abroad (1980) 85
Abyssinia, Italian invasion of 98
aerial bombing
   bombsites as "waste lands" 124–30
   history of 136
   imagery in war travel books 100–1
Africa
   colonization in 4
African Americans, violence against 3–4
airplane, weaponization of 136
Alamein to Zem Zem 105
Albania 3
Alexander, Michael 112
Allen, Nicholas 80
American Civil War 24–5
"An Indiscreet Journey" 40

Anderson, Benedict 76
anthropology, domestic 88
anxiety 28, 66, 72, 107, 120, 137–8
apocalypse 26–32, 135–6
"apolitical unconscious" of 1930s writing 89
appeasement, government's policy of 106
Arms and the Man (1894) 24
At Lady Molly's (1960) 99–100
At the Violet Hour (2012) 5, 16, 37, 62, 66–7, 127
atomic bombing, 135–40
Atonement (2001) 110
Auden, W. H. 24, 33, 61, 62, 85, 87, 90–1, 92, 97
   emigration to United States 100
"Auden Generation, the" 87, 91, 97
autobiography 91, 114–15
"Autumn on Nan-Yüeh" (1940) 89–90

Back (1946) 120–2
Barnhisel, Greg 133–4
Beasley, Rebecca 68
Beauchamp, Leslie 40, 42
Beckett, Samuel 2, 80, 112, 130, 131, 135
Beer, Gillian 137
belle époque myth 8
Benjamin, Walter 36–7
Bergonzi, Bernard 11, 28, 35, 125
Berman, Jessica 92, 95
Bernstein, Michael André 48–9

Between the Acts (1941) 88, 103, 112, 137, 138
Black Lamb and Grey Falcon 98
Black Mischief (1932) 98–9
BLAST 15, 47, 53, 56
Blasting and Bombardiering 1, 6–7, 35–6, 106
Blitz 118–28, 137–8
  "myth" 124
  "Blitz spirit" 124
  "Blitz sublime" 128
Bluemel, Kristin 86–7
Body in Pain, The (1985) 55
Boehmer, Elleke 5
Boer War 19–22
Bolshevik Revolution 68
bombing 3, 70–1, 100–1, 105, 115, 118–20, 136–8
  atomic 29
  bombsites as "waste lands" 125–30
  suicide 66, 72, 75
  visual recording of 94–5, 137
bombsites 124–30
Booth, Allyson 12–13, 16, 42–3
Bourke, Joanna 25
Bowen, Elizabeth 33, 81–3, 87, 113, 116–17, 122–4, 125–6, 135
Bowen's Court (1940) 126
"Break of Day in the Trenches" 7
Brearton, Fran 75–9
"Britain in Autumn" (1940) 124
British Literature of the Blitz (2009) 120–1
British Writers and the Approach of World War II (2015) 138
British Writers of the Thirties (1988) 91
British Writing of the Second World War (2000) 126
Brooke, Rupert 15
"Brother Fire" 120
Buch, Robert 62

Calder, Angus 124
Campbell, James 10–11
Camus, Albert 29
Carol (King) 3
Cather, Willa 46
Caught (1943) 115–19
Cavell, Edith 93
Céline, Louis-Ferdinand 56
Chamberlain, Neville 95
"Channel Firing" 2
Chesterton, G. K. 64
childhood
  children as victims 76, 94
  experience of war 114, 127, 130
  trauma associated with 119, 130
China 89–91
civilians 20, 22, 38–40, 56, 120, 122–3
  and aerial bombing 136–9
  incomprehensibility of combat experience to 9–10
Clewell, Tammy 51, 54
Clymer, Jeffory A. 64
Cohen, Debra Rae 46
Cold War
  and atomic bombing 135–40
  late modernism as product of 1, 33–4, 132–3
Cold War Modernists (2015) 133–4
Cole, Sarah 5, 16, 26, 37, 62, 66–7, 121
"colonial bombsite" 136
colonization, in Africa 4
"combat gnosticism" 10
Coming Up For Air (1939) 106, 138–9
Command of the Air, The (1921) 139
Committed Styles (2014) 89
Congress for Cultural Freedom 134
Connolly, Cyril 29–30, 97, 103–4, 109–10

Conrad in the Twenty-First Century (2005) 65–6
Conrad, Joseph 18
  analogy between writing and terrorism 63, 65–6
  commonalities with H. G. Wells 30–1
  depiction of violence 26–7, 141
  timeliness of 65
Cooper, John Xiros 133
Crane, Stephen 24–5
Culture in Camouflage (2009) 109
Cunard, Nancy 3–4, 97
Cunningham, Valentine 91–2
Czechoslovakia 98

Daly, Nicholas 26
Darrohn, Christine 42
"Daughters of the Late Colonel" 41–2
Davis, Thomas S. 6, 87–8, 92, 126, 139
Day Lewis, Cecil 110
dead body, prevalence of in modernist writing 13, 40–2, 83, 94, 126, 137–8
Death in Life (1945) 135
"Death Valley" 21
Death, Men, and Modernism (2003) 41
decolonization 88
DeCoste, Damon Marcel 121
Deer, Patrick 109, 116, 121
"delayed decoding" 70
Demon Lover, The 122, 126
Derrida, Jacques 139–40
"Desert Flowers" 104
deserters 59
disfigurement, physical 25
documentary 12, 29, 86, 88–9, 94
  "culture" 88–9
  as object of suspicion 95–6
Doolittle, Hilda 112
Douglas, Keith 21, 104–5

Douhet, Guilio 139
Down and Out in Paris and London 100
"Drummer Hodge" 21
dynamite 3, 63–4, 66, 72, 81
Dynamiter, The (1885) 64, 71

Easter Rising (1916) 62, 74–5
Einhaus, Ann-Marie 39–40
Eksteins, Modris 14, 16, 38
Eliot, T. S.
  later poetry 33, 56–7, 87, 103, 112, 119, 123, 127–9, 133
  response to First World War 5, 7, 11, 20, 45, 54–5, 83, 87
Ellis, Steve 87, 138
Ellmann, Maud 54
Empson, William 33, 89–90
Endgame (1957) 135
Enemies of Promise (1938) 29
English Eliot, The (1991) 87
Esty, Jed 4
Europe to Let (1940) 98
Extinct Scene, The: Late Modernism and Everyday Life (2015) 6, 87

fascism 30, 86, 87, 92–3, 96, 97, 98, 107, 111
Faulkner, William 8, 13
feminism 46–7, 48, 96
"Fenian" bombings 75
fire
  associated with trauma 117–19
  firemen 115
  and psychological revelation 119–20
  war as purification by 120
"Fireman Flower" 119
firemen 115
First World War 1, 5–6
  as bodily violence 55
  cultural repercussions of 14, 17, 22–3, 37–8, 45–6

deserters 59
  as emancipation 14–15
  futility of 19–20, 56, 106
  incomplete displacement of 12–13, 42–3
  and Ireland 78–9
  literary afterlife of 56–60
  revival of traditional forms 17
  Second World War in relation to 105–6, 114, 121–2
  as testing ground for masculinity 53
Fitzgerald, Scott F. 8, 13
Fitzgibbon, Constantine 138
"Fly, The" 44–5
For Whom the Bell Tolls (1940) 92
Ford Foundation 134
Ford, Madox Ford 18, 47, 53–4
foreshadowing 48–9
Fort, The (1941) 122
Four Quartets (1943) 112, 133
Franco (General) 3, 92
Frazer, James 14
Freedman, Ariela 41
Freud, Sigmund 43–4, 55, 121
From Ritual to Romance (1920) 14
Fussell, Paul 10–11, 17, 31–2, 38–9, 57, 85, 103, 110

Gance, Abel 106
Gandal, Keith 8
"Garden Party, The" 42
Genter, Robert 133
George, David Lloyd 106
Germany 3, 90
Gibbon, Lewis Grassic 58–9, 138
Golden Bough, The (1890) 14
Good Soldier, The (1915) 53–4
Goodbye to Berlin (1939) 88, 90
Grass, Günter 130
Grausam, Daniel 140
Great Gatsby, The (1925) 13

Great War and Modern Memory (1975) 10–11
Great War and the Language of Modernism, The (2003) 6, 38–9
Great War, the *see* First World War
Green, Henry 33, 100–1, 113–22, 137
Greene, Graham 86, 116, 120–1
Guernica 137
guilt
  war 45, 106, 114–15
Gurney, Ivor 9

"Haidekampf" 55
Hara, Tamiki 29, 116
Hardy, Thomas 2, 19–20, 21
Heart of Darkness (1899) 27, 30–1, 72
Heartbreak House (1919) 15
Heat of the Day, The (1949) 116–17, 122–4, 135
Hemingway, Ernest 8, 25, 33, 52, 92, 132
Heroes' Twilight 11, 28
Hewison, Robert 100
Hillary, Richard 87
Hiroshima 29, 135
Hitler, Adolf 3, 95, 108, 111
Ho, Janice 6
Hochschild, Adam 59
Holocaust 5
"Homage to a Government" 62
Homage to Catalonia (1938) 91, 100
Horizon 97, 104, 109–10
Houen, Alex 63, 70, 72
Hugh Selwyn Mauberley (1920) 7, 10
Hulme, T. E. 7
Hynes, Samuel 23, 45–6, 97

Imagination at War (1995) 104
imperialism 26–8

In a Strange Room (2014) 40–1
In Parenthesis 56–8
influenza pandemic 40
"Informer, The" (1906) 70–1
"Inside the Whale" 106–9
intermodernism 86–7
interwar literature
   documentary movement 88–9
   generational pathology 91
   political detachment 89–90
   and political engagement in 87
   Spanish Civil War, *see as main heading*
   symbolization of foreign wars 93–4
   war travel books *see as main heading*
Inventing Ireland (1995) 76
IRA 74
Ireland
   allure of violence 77–8
   decolonization in 5
   divided political loyalties 81–2
   Easter Rising (1916) 62, 74–5
   "Fenian" bombings 75
   First World War 78–9
   IRA 74
   nationalism as religion 76
   sacrificial language for struggle 76–7
irony 72–3
Isherwood, Christopher 33, 85, 88, 90–1, 98
   emigration to United States 100
"Island and the Aeroplane, The" 137
Island of Dr Moreau, The (1896) 30
Italy 3
Ivens, Joris 92
Ivory Tower 97, 111

J'Accuse (1919) 106
Jacob's Room (1922) 9, 48–9

James, Henry 18, 33, 63, 88, 100, 113–14, 116
James, Pearl 13
Jameson, Fredric 34, 87, 98, 122, 132–3
Jameson, Storm 34, 87, 98, 122
Jeffery, Keith 79
Jones, David 56–8
Jordan, Heather Bryant 81
"journalistic," style of writing 16–17, 29–30, 68–9
Journey to a War (1939) 90–1
Journey to the End of the Night (1932) 56
Joyce, James 7, 11, 16, 57, 80, 131, 132, 140
Juno and the Paycock (1924) 74–5

Kaplan, Carola M. 66
Katherine Mansfield Studies 40
Kendall, Tim 20, 24, 122
Keyes, Sydney 128
Kiberd, Declan 76–8
Kipling, Rudyard 20, 22–4, 31, 32
Knowles, Sebastian D. G. A. 119
Kohlmann, Benjamin 89
Kristine Miller 120–1

Lady Chatterley's Lover (1928) 38–9
Larkin, Philip 62
Lassner, Phyllis 81
Last Enemy, The (1942) 87
Last September, The (1929) 81–3, 126
Late Imperial Romance (1994) 27
Late Modernism: Art, Culture, and Politics in Cold War America (2010) 133
Late Modernism: Politics, Fiction, and the Arts between

INDEX

the World Wars (1999) 129–30, 135–6
"late modernism" 130
  assumptions of 134
  atomic bombing, 135–40
  "mid-century" 135
  as product of Cold War 132–3
  see also second-wave modernism
Lawrence, D. H. 11, 16, 25–6, 38–9, 40, 132
"Leaning Tower, The" (1940) 97, 106
Leed, Eric 53
Lehmann, John 132
Levenback, Karen L. 50
Levenson, Michael 130
Lewis, C. S. 119
Lewis, Pericles 62
Lewis, Wyndham 1, 35–6, 47, 106, 141
  BLAST 15
  "Men of 1914" 6–7, 9
Liddell, Robert 127
"Life of Ma Parker" 41
Lifton, Robert Jay 135
Lion, the Witch and the Wardrobe, The (1950) 119
"Little Gidding" 20
London, Modernism, and 1914 (2010) 8–9
Lord Jim (1902) 26
"Lost Generation" 8
Love, the Reward (1885) 69

Macaulay, Rose 127–8
Maclean, Caroline 68
MacLean, Sorley 21
MacNeice, Louis 120
Mallios, Peter Lancelot 21, 120
"Man He Killed, The" 19–20
Man Who Was Thursday, The (1908) 64
"mandarin," style of writing 29

Mansfield, Katherine 40–3
  criticism of *Night and Day* (1919) 49
  loss of brother 40, 42
Marcus, Laura 88–9
Marx, John 4, 66, 120
masculinity 26–7, 41, 46–8, 52–3, 120–1
Mass Observation project 88
May, Philip 69
McClure, John A. 27
McEwan, Ian 110
McHale, Brian 65
McNulty, Eugene 27, 78
Mellor, Leo 101, 125, 136, 138
"Men of 1914" 7, 9
"mid-century" 135
Middleton, Peter 20, 43
migration, mass 88
Miller, Henry 109
Miller, Tyrus 88–9, 129–30, 135–6
Ministry of Fear, The 120
"Modern Fiction" 28
Modernism and World War II (2007) 134
modernism
  apolitical 108–9
  definitions of 17–18
  and documentary 88–9
  and history 11–12
  prewar conceptions of 18
  recidivism 110
  second-wave 111–24
    revisionist dimension 112–13
    "second generation" modernists 113–14
Modernism, Media, and Propaganda (2006) 6
Moore, George 81, 88
Mortality and Form in Late Modernist Literature (2014) 112–13
Morton, Stephen 5

Mr Britling Sees it Through
   (1916) 35
Mrs Dalloway 20, 26, 32, 50
Muldoon, Paul 76
Munich Agreement 138
Murry, John Middleton 43
Musil, Robert 48
Mussolini, Benito 3
"Mysterious Kôr" 125–6

Nabokov, Vladimir 130, 132
Nagasaki 135
Nation and Citizenship in the Twentieth-Century British Novel 6
nationalism, as religion 76
Nazism 21, 90, 111, 130
Negro (1934) 3
New Signatures 89
New Writing in Europe (1940) 132
Newton, Michael 75
Nichols, Bill 89
Night and Day (1919) 49
"Nineteen Hundred and Nineteen" 74
"No Apocalypse, Not Now (Full Speed Ahead, Seven Missiles, Seven Missives)" (1984) 139–40
Nobel, Alfred 3
Norris, Margot 10, 30, 55, 132
Notes Toward a Definition of Culture (1948) 133
"nuclear criticism" 139–40
nuclear war 135–40

Ó Donghaile, Deaglán 63
O'Casey, Sean 25, 74–5, 78–9, 80
October Revolution 68
"On Transience" 43–4
Orwell, George 33, 37–8, 91, 93–4, 100, 106–9, 139
Ouditt, Sharon 46

Outka, Elizabeth 40
Owen, Wilfred 9–11, 20–1, 33, 41, 45, 79, 81–2, 87–8, 105

"pacification" 28
pacifism 27–8, 33, 48, 56, 93–4, 106, 136
Pack My Bag (1940) 114–15
"Parable of the Old Man and the Young, The" 45
Parade's End 54
Parkes, Adam 67, 70
Party Going 100–1, 137
Passos, John Dos 92
Pathos of the Real, The (2010) 62
Peace Pledge Union 106
photographs, war, *see* photojournalism
photojournalism 94–5, 137
Picasso, Pablo 137
Piette, Adam 104
Pilsudski (General) 3
Pisan Cantos (1948) 112
Plague, The (1947) 29
Playboy of the Western World, The (1907) 77
Plotting Terror (2001) 63
Plough and the Stars, The (1926) 76, 80
Plunkett, Joseph 76
"Poets in this War" 104–5
Poland 3
Postcards from the Trenches (1996) 12–13, 42–3
Postmodernist Fiction (1987) 65
postwar life
   belatedness of trauma 52
   culture of emotional repression 36–7, 50–3
   official mourning 51
Pound, Ezra 7, 10–11, 15–16, 33, 112–13
Powell, Anthony 76, 99–100

Princess Casamassima, The (1886) 63, 65
propaganda 95–6
Prussian Officer, The (1914) 25–6
psychiatric damage 24–6
psychoanalysis 120
Puchner, Martin 64, 66
Put Out More Flags (1942) 111

Radicals on the Road (2001) 98
Rae, Patricia 54
Raitt, Suzanne 46
Rau, Petra 4
Rawlinson, Mark 126
Read, Herbert 12, 105
Reading the Ruins: Modernism, Bombsites and British Culture (2011) 125
Red Badge of Courage, The (1895) 24–5
Reed, John 41, 68–9
Regarding the Pain of Others (2003) 94–5
Rites of Spring: The Great War and the Birth of the Modern Age (1989) 14
Rogers, Gayle 92, 95–6
Romania 3
Rosenberg, Isaac 7, 9, 104
Ross Bullock, Philip 68, 143
Roth, Joseph 40, 42, 48, 49
Russian Revolution 3, 64, 68

Saint-Amour, Paul K. 28–9, 136, 139, 141
Sansom, William 119
Sartoris (1929) 13
Sassoon, Siegfried 9–11, 23
Scanlan, Margaret 63
Scarry, Elaine 55
Schweitzer, Bernard 98
Scoop (1938) 98–9
Scottsboro 4

second-wave modernism 33, 105, 111–24
see also late-modernism
Second World War 5–6, 88
   destabilization of Britain's superpower status 6
   literature of
      in comparison to First World War 103–4
      psychoanalysis 120
      soldier poets 104–5
   modernism in 105, 112, 121–2
   in relation to First World War 105–6, 114, 121–2
Secret Agent, The (1907) 30, 63, 65–8, 73–4
Seiler, Claire 135, 137
Selassie, Haile 98
Serbo-Bulgarian war (1885) 24
"Shadow in the Rose Garden, The" 25
Shadow of a Gunman, The (1923) 76, 78
Shaw, George Bernard 15, 24
shell shock 120–2
Sherman, David 40–1
Sherry, Vincent 6–7, 17–18, 36
short story 39–40
Showalter, Elaine 53
Sillars, Stuart 128
Silver Tassie, The (1928) 79–80
Sino-Japanese War 87
Sites of Memory, Sites of Mourning (1995) 17
"Sixteen Dead Men" 74
Smith, Angela K. 46
"Soldier's Home" (1925) 52
Sontag, Susan 94–5
Sorley, Charles 54
South Africa, Boer War 19–20
"Spain" 92
Spanish Civil War 87–8, 91–6

canonization of 92
historic importance of 91–2
photojournalism 94–5
symbolization of 93–4
Spanish Earth, The (1937) 92
Spender, Stephen 97
"Spilling the Spanish Beans" 94
Stalin, Joseph 3, 111
Stamboul Train (1932) 86
Stansky, Peter 138
Stein, Gertrude 8
Stevens, Wallace 113
Stevenson, Robert Louis 64
Stites, Richard 3
Stonebridge, Lyndsey 120
"Storyteller, The" (1936) 36
Stramm, August 55
Stravinsky, Igor 14
"Summer Flower" (1945) 29
Sunset Song (1932) 58–9
surrealism 88
Sword of Honour (1952–61)
 110–11, 128–9
Synge, J. M. 15, 77–8

Tate, Trudi 13, 46
Taylor, Antony 3, 66
Ten Days that Shook the World
 (1919) 68–9
Tense Future (1922) 136
Terrorism and Modern Literature
 (2002) 63
terrorism, narratives of 2–5, 64–7,
 72–6
 clichés as target 68
 The Secret Agent (1907) *see as
  main heading*
Thomas, Dylan 103
Three Guineas (1938) 93–4,
 121, 137
Tin Drum, The (1959) 130
To the Lighthouse (1927)
 13–14, 50

total war 136–7
totalitarianism 3, 109
travel book, war
 China 90–1
 clichés 99
 Czechoslovakia 98
 imagery of aerial bombing 100–1
 insecurity of civilian life 87–8
 political detachment 89–90
 politics 98
 pro-Fascist 98
 as war reportage 85–6
Treglown, Jeremy 100
*Truth about the Peace Treaties,
 The* 106

Ulysses 9
Under Western Eyes (1911) 65, 68,
 69, 71–2
United States Information
 Agency 134
United States
 American Civil War 24–5
 violence against African
  Americans 3–4
Unreal City (1952) 127

Vera, or the Nihilists (1882) 75
"*Vergissmeinnicht*" 21
violence 26–9, 37
 bodily 55
 as form of political
  expression 67
 and poetry 77–8
 and socialization of
  young men 48
Virginia Woolf and the Great War
 (1999) 50
Virginia Woolf and War (1991) 50

Walls Do Not Fall, The (1944) 112
Walsh, Michael 8–9
"war books boom" 38

War of the Worlds, The (1897) 27–32, 54
Waste Land, The (1922) 5, 9, 20, 45, 54–5, 123, 127, 136
Watt (1953) 112
Watt, Ian 70
Waugh in Abyssinia (1936) 98
Waugh, Evelyn 31, 33, 86, 97–9, 110–11, 128–9
Wells, H. G. 54–5, 64, 117
  commonalities with Joseph Conrad 30–1
  violence 27–32
West, Rebecca 26, 46, 68, 87, 98
Weston, Jesse 14
Whittier-Ferguson, John 112–13
"Why I Write" 107–8
"Widow's Party, The" 23
Wilde, Oscar 64–5, 75, 77, 90
Will, Barbara 75, 112
Winter, Jay
  cultural repercussions of First World War 17–18, 54
Wollaeger, Mark 6, 72
women's responses, to First World War 46–8

Wood, Michael 74
Woolf, Virginia 9, 13–14, 26, 28, 29, 32, 121, 138
  as feminist 16, 48, 96
  pacifism 33, 48, 56, 93–4
  proposal for "Outsiders Society" 94
  second-wave modernism 112–13
  Spanish Civil War 88, 92–6, 137
Woolfs' Hogarth Press 12, 114, 119
World My Wilderness, The (1949) 127–8
Writing War in the Twentieth Century (2000) 10

Years, The (1937) 88, 93
Yeats, W. B. 10, 11, 15
  association with violence 74
  and Ireland 74, 76–7, 79, 83–4
Yugoslavia 98

Zog (King) 3

www.ingramcontent.com/pod-product-compliance
Lightning Source LLC
Chambersburg PA
CBHW050140240426
43673CB00043B/1741